Looking at Sails

Looking at Sails

Bruce Banks and Dick Kenny

Illustrated by Peter Campbell

Photographs by Alastair Black,
John Blomfield and Others

First published in the United States 1979 by
SAIL BOOKS, INC.
38 Commercial Wharf,
Boston, Massachusetts 02110

ISBN 0-914814-21-4

Distributed to bookstores by
W. W. Norton & Co. Inc.

Printed in Italy
by Officine Grafiche F.lli Stianti - Sancasciano - Florence

Contents

Photographic credits:
Most of the photographs reproduced were taken by Alastair Black,
John Blomfield or Dick Kenny. Others are the work of Beken of Cowes,
Bob Fisher, Roger Smith, Bruce Banks, Eric North and Bitterne
Photographic.

Acknowledgements

While the art of sailing remains as yesteryear, the science changes and develops at an ever increasing pace. New materials demand new techniques which in turn spawn new materials. Nowhere is this as true as in the field of sailmaking which these days can be more accurately termed fabric engineering.

It would have been impossible to paint an accurate and comprehensive picture of these developments without the generous help of a number of persons at Bruce Banks Sails Limited, especially Ken Rose, technical and design director. Among specialists within the Sarisbury loft who gave their advice and time willingly were Colin Merrett, Peter Bateman and Eddy Warden Owen.

Two outside specialists, equally as willing and helpful, were Paul Nevard of Richard Hayward & Sons, sailcloth weavers, Crewkerne, and Colin Turner of Lewmar Marine, winch manufacturers, Havant.

Without willing crews on numerous boats the pictures would still be in the imagination, so thank you to John, Don, Mike and David.

To Lesley and Rosemary for advice and patience, thank you; the same to Linda Watson and Diana Tamplin for typing the text and collecting pictures.

Our appreciation of the skills of illustrator Peter Campbell, and photographers Alastair Black and John Blomfield is obviously displayed on the pages that follow. However, their application and goodwill outside the call of creative duty were outstanding.

Only the weather gets no thanks. It was never right.

B.B.
D.K.

1 Theory

Introduction

To the sailmaker there seems to be no happy medium. For him the search for the perfect sail is likely to be an all-consuming passion, and naturally he finds it difficult to understand why this quest is not shared by the vast majority of sailors who use his products. At the other end of the scale there are the minority who, appreciating the importance of their sails, never give him a minute's peace.

A case overstated? Well, maybe. But one thing is certain. To every sailor, whatever his degree of skill, a better understanding of sails is the key to a massive increase in his enjoyment of sailing.

That simply is the aim of this book. To help the reader to look at his sails and appreciate what he or she is seeing. That in the end is the only answer. Sailing is thankfully still more of an art than a science and, while it remains so, no handbook in the world is going to bestow instant success. Sails do not hide their secrets. The answers are there for all to see—it is merely a question of knowing how to read them.

Seam reading

Luckily in this reading lesson the sailor has one thing on his side. Sails are—contrary to first appearances—not featureless expanses of cloth. They have seams, and it is these that provide the picture (fig 1-1). Throughout the book we will be returning to this theme. Learn to read the seams; they will tell you exactly what is going on and whether you have got it right or wrong.

Having said sailing is still mainly an art, it may seem an about face to then plunge into the realms of aerodynamics and physics. Don't be put off, it is not going to last for long.

However, it is essential to anyone interested in sails, and indeed sailing, that the fundamental principles are thoroughly understood.

To the non-sailor, unconcerned with the mysteries of why a boat can sail into the wind, the answer is simple. Offer a broad surface to the wind and it will push you along. Wrong. Even when we come later to look at spinnakers, this is only a part of the truth.

No, the conversion of wind power into forward drive for the boat is dependent on three elements, all of which have to work in harmony. This is true on all points of sailing, but is at its most dramatic when going to windward. It is on this point that we shall therefore concentrate.

fig 1-1

The airfoil

Think of the wind as a mass of air moving along parallel lines (fig 1-2). When a curved obstruction is introduced into that flow the air is forced to separate; the upper flow having to travel further around the curved top of the obstacle, than that over the lower surface.

Two laws of physics now enter the picture.

Because the deflected lines of flow have to travel further, they speed up; and in so doing the air becomes less dense (Bernoulli's Law). At the same time these deflected lines are being compressed between the obstruction—or airfoil—and the undisturbed straight lines of air flow above them. This compression accelerates the flow (Venturi's Law) which in turn reduces even further the density of air above the obstruction. With less pressure above it, the airfoil is drawn up into the partial vacuum.

Hold a table-spoon lightly between finger and thumb, with the curved back of the spoon close to running water (fig 1-3(a)). As the curved surface touches the water stream (b) you will feel the jerk as the spoon is pulled into the flow.

fig 1-2

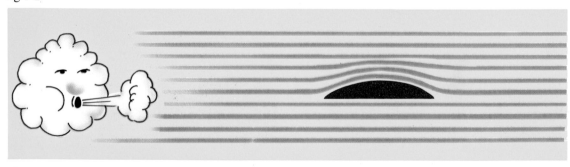

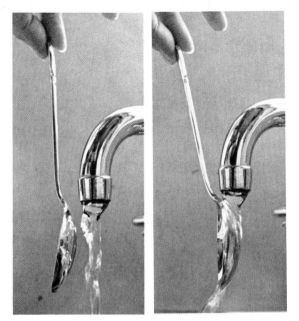

fig 1-3(a)   fig 1-3(b)

1-4). The flow is then caught in the windward surface forcing the sail into an airfoil section. Once this has been achieved the flow around the curved leeward surface begins its familiar acceleration, drawing the sail towards the lower pressure area (fig 1-5).

The concave—or windward—surface of the sail, which initially caught the wind is also having its effect on the flow. Whereas our earlier obstruction (fig 1-2) had a flat lower surface, now we have a space on the windward side of the sail. To fill this gap in the forward part of the sail, the airflow has to move more slowly than that still travelling in straight lines alongside it. Here Bernoulli's Law

fig 1-4, fig 1-5

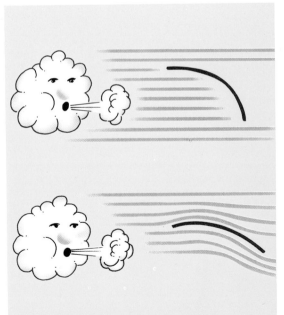

To anyone unfamiliar with some of the disciplines of the scientific world this may not appear too convincing. Let us reassure you. The power generated by flow over an airfoil is sufficient to hold a 300 ton jumbo jetliner up in the sky quite successfully.

However, unlike the pilot whose aircraft wings are already shaped to provide lift, the sailor has only a flat expanse of cloth. Edge this directly into the wind: the flow and pressure will remain the same on both sides and the sail will merely flap.

Before the sail can begin to convert the wind into power for the boat, it has to use that same wind to give it the necessary shape.

To achieve this somewhat deceitful aim, the sail must be presented to the windflow at an angle (fig

works in reverse; as the flow slows down, pressure builds up and consolidates the airfoil shape.

The sail, having manipulated the flow into providing the necessary shape, is now in a position to convert that flow into movement for the boat.

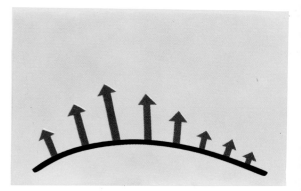

fig 1-6

The amount of that power and its direction is however dependent on the curvature of the sail over which the air is flowing. The greater the curvature, the greater the force generated. Over the deepest part of the curve, the flow, both to leeward and windward, is producing relatively more power than over the flatter surfaces fore and aft. The direction of the force generated is perpendicular to the direction of airflow, so that at any point on the curve it can be illustrated (fig 1-6) both in strength—length of arrow—and direction. For the sake of clarity all of these little arrows can then be combined into one large one (fig 1-7), representing the total force available, and its direction.

The third element in the process lies with the boat. The power transmitted from the sails so far is largely sideways. However, the shape of any hull, aided by either centreboard or keel, is designed to resist sideways movement and go forward. The leeward force is therefore resisted—and the boat

fig 1-7

12

fig 1-8

goes in the direction of least resistance. The
amount of power available to move the boat
forward can be clearly seen (fig. 1-8), if the total
force (red) is broken into sideways (yellow) and
forward (green) components relative to the boat's
centreline.

Immediately it becomes apparent that when
sailing close hauled, the amount of forward drive
power is relatively minute. It becomes even more
precious when we take into account the drag
induced by friction over the sails and rig, and that
caused by the hull through the water.

It is also obvious that everything possible must be
done to help the boat resist the large sideways
force. This relationship between the direction of

available power from the sail and the relative direction of the boat is underlined by looking at what happens when the boat turns away from the wind (fig 1-9).

The wind direction and the angle at which the sails are presented are the same. In this diagram the curvature of the sail also remains the same, so that both sails are generating similar forces (red). However, when this is now resolved into forward and sideways elements related to the direction of the boat, a very different picture emerges.

As the boat points progressively away from the wind direction so a greater proportion of the sail is developing forward (green) drive. The result we all

fig 1-10

know from experience. Less sideways force allows the boat to come upright, and more forward force increases the speed.

By retaining the same imaginary sail shape we can now illustrate the importance of presenting the sail at the correct angle to the wind, relative to the direction of travel (fig 1-10).

Imagine that this sail is generating the same power as that in (fig 1-9). To helmsman and crew the sails on both may look similar, but what a difference there is in the forward and sideways forces being generated.

In reality these two sails could never produce equal power, because the sail in fig 1-9 is being presented to the wind at too coarse an angle. Airflow travels in straight lines. Ask it to bend too sharply and it will ignore you. The flow disengages from the leeside of the sail (fig 1-11) and is replaced

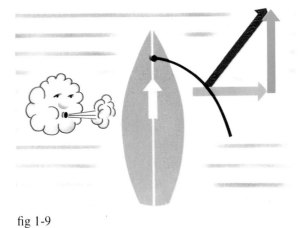

fig 1-9

14

with turbulence—the classic stall. To windward, pressure is however building up, although even there the flow is restricted. The sail looks all right, but power is lacking; and as we have shown above, too great a proportion of what little there is, is sideways force.

Taking things to the other extreme, what is the effect if the sail is presented at too fine an angle to the wind? Now the flow on the windward side is being asked to bend too sharply (fig 1–12).

fig 1-11

Without the necessary pressure forming on the concave side there is insufficient substance in the sail to deflect the windward flow from its straight path and the curve collapses into a flutter.

At least when this happens the sailor is given due notice; the luff of the sail caves in. But both examples illustrate the importance of presenting the sail at the correct—and if one is talking of sailing fast, we mean precisely correct (fig 1-13)— angle to the wind. (See page 16)

Having examined the relationship between the wind, the angle of the sail, and the forward movement of the boat, let us now delve a little more deeply into what happens to the flow passing over the sail surface, and the effects of varying depths of camber.

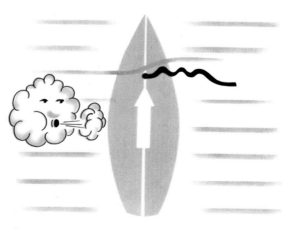

fig 1-12

Shape

Earlier we looked at the basic curve and saw how it generated power from the wind. Flow over the forward windward surface slowed down providing the necessary pressure to produce an airfoil, which in turn accelerated the flow to leeward reducing pressure and thereby generating motive power. That however is not the whole story. Look again at the curve (fig 1–14).

Once the fast moving leeward airflow is past the point of deepest curvature, the flow lines are diverging from the unaffected lines above them. The flow over the after part of the leeward surface, although it must therefore be slowing down, is still moving more quickly than the surrounding air. Over the windward surface after an initial slowing down the flow is being quite rigourously compres-

fig 1-13

fig 1-14

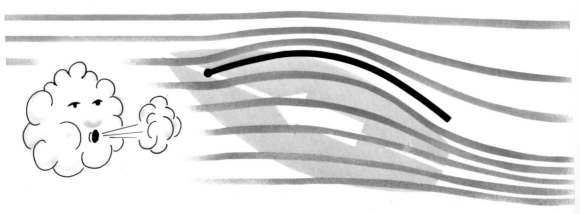

fig 1-15

sed between the aft end of the sail and the undisturbed flow lines below it. By the time it reaches the flat surface of the leech this flow is developing the same momentum as its counterpart to leeward. They exit the sail together, and because they are travelling faster than the free air aft of the sail, they react by pushing the sail forward. This exhaust works in exactly the same way as a jet engine. It is not the primary source of power, but rather, a useful auxiliary; and is a direct result of the long flat leech sections familiar on all fore and aft rigs today, and unheard of by the square sail sailors two centuries ago.

Apparent wind

As the boat moves forward, another factor enters the picture, contributing further to the dynamic generation of power by the sails reacting to the wind.

Stand still in a 3 knot wind and that is what you feel on your face (fig 1-15). Run into it at 3 knots and the speed increases *relative to you* to 6 knots. Retreat from the wind at 3 knots and the breeze disappears. When a boat is sailing towards the wind, that wind increases in direct relation to the vessel's speed.

17

The difference between the true and apparent speeds adds naturally to the velocity of the flows being generated on both surfaces of the sail. However, as the surrounding airflow remains true, the 'apparent' flow exhausting off the leech is travelling again just that little bit faster.

Before leaving apparent wind let us look at how forward boat movement affects the angle of the wind as well as its speed (fig 1-16). On the left the true wind velocity (blue line) is 6 knots and its direction 293°. The boat is moving due north at 3 knots (yellow line). By finding the third side of a simple triangle of velocities we see that when the wind meets the boat it has a speed of 7.66 knots, and has changed direction forward to 314°. Assuming the same boat speed but with the true wind on the right blowing at 6 knots from a point abaft the beam of 113° we see that its apparent speed has decreased to 5.5 knots, but that the apparent wind direction has still moved forward to 083°.

Remember these *apparent* wind angles and speeds are the only ones that matter when it comes to sail trim.

fig 1-16

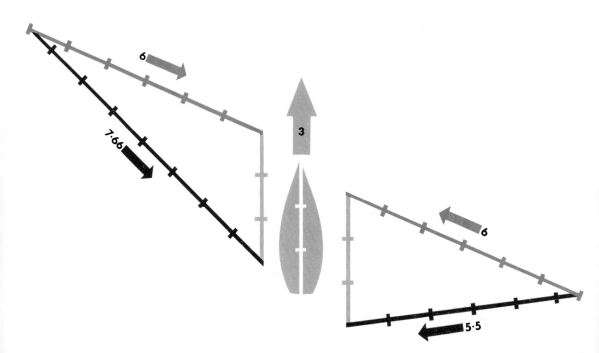

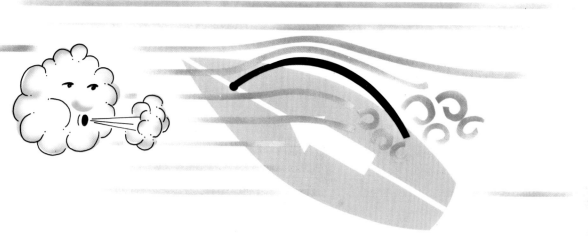

fig 1-17

Camber

It has become evident that the amount of power which can be generated by any sail is controlled (a) by the speed of the wind, and (b) by the degree to which that flow can be deflected.

Why not, you may ask, have every sail with a large depth of camber? More camber; more deflection; more power. The answer lies in the strength of the wind. If the depth of the camber is too deep for the wind speed (fig 1-17), the contour-following flow to windward becomes trapped by the fast moving unaffected straight lines and consequently pressure builds up on the aft windward surface of the sail. To leeward the flow follows the camber over the fore part of the sail but then the curve becomes too great and the wind rejoins its fast flowing neighbours. More wind could cause the forward side of the curve to collapse entirely.

The answer is to flatten the camber. A flatter section working efficiently produces far more drive than a powerful section over which the flow has, even partially, broken down.

Interestingly, flow can also break down if the camber is too great for very light wind. In a slow moving airstream there is not enough momentum to keep the flow attached to the surface of the sail. Again the answer is to flatten the depth of camber.

19

has got, that hockey ball will go a great deal further than it will when driven by the stronger player on his own.

The two sails work together in exactly the same way. Although there are now two similar obstructions, each deflecting the airflow lines and producing power in its own right, the sum total of drive generated by both working as a team is far greater.

Earlier we saw how the deflected flow over the leeward sail surface was accelerated by compression against the adjacent straight lines of undisturbed air. The introduction (fig 1-19) of a foresail (green) provides a more substantial wall to the deflected flow over the lee of the red mainsail. A considerably faster flow is generated both across the power producing lee of the red sail, and against the relatively slower surrounding air.

fig 1-18

Sail interaction

Before turning from theory to practice, let's take a final step towards the real thing and add a second sail to the plan.

Sailors of cat-rigged boats such as Finns and Sunfish can skip this bit.

A headsail and mainsail working together (fig 1-18) produce more power than a mainsail alone, even though it be equal to their combined areas.

Imagine a contest between, on the one hand, a 200 pound hockey player, and on the other a father and son team whose combined weights equal the same. The purpose being to hit the ball furthest. If the son hits the ball first, so that it is already moving fast by the time it passes the father, and he gives the speeding projectile all he

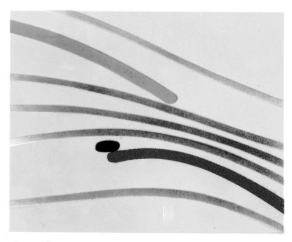

fig 1-19

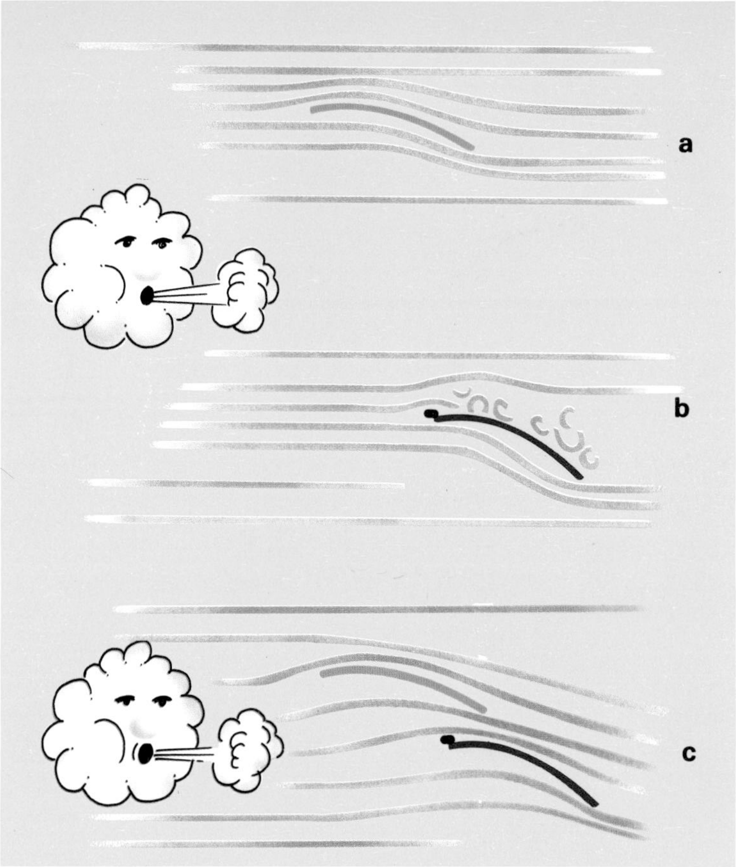

fig 1-20

On its own the forward lee surface of the mainsail will be shadowed from the flow by the mast section causing turbulence. The accelerated flow from the headsail smoothes out this turbulence, redirecting flow across this important section of the mainsail.

The further benefit from this redirection of flow from one sail to the other is that it allows the main to be sheeted much closer to the centreline of the

fig 1-21

boat, creating greater acceleration of wind without the flow breaking away to leeward (fig 1-20).

In (a) we see the green headsail sheeted correctly for a given windspeed. Flow is attached along the full length of both surfaces.

In (b) the flow on the after lee surface of the red mainsail has broken away. Either the depth of camber is too great for the airflow; or the sail is oversheeted. To reattach the flow to a single sail would mean either flattening the camber or easing the sheet; in both cases producing less power. In (c) green and red are working as one, and neither action is necessary. Although the respective sail camber and angles are identical to those in (a) and (b), the flow is now turned in by green towards the lee surface of red. This then is the effect to be achieved from the all important slot. Producing it, in a wide variety of conditions, is one of the more demanding practical challenges facing sailmaker and sailor alike.

The slot

At its most efficient, the gap—or slot—must be of even taper, extending from the head of the foresail down to the point where one sail no longer has an effect on its partner.

If at any point this horizontal gap becomes too narrow, the accelerating flow leaving the first sail is trapped (fig 1-21). This air, building up pressure, forces the mainsail luff to windward (back winding) causing turbulence on the leech of the headsail and denying the windward surface of the mainsail luff, the opportunity to build positive pressure.

The constriction of flow around too narrow a slot also starves the flow over the lee surface of the main. Consequently the flow over the whole lee of the rig, aft from the point of greatest depth of camber on the headsail, is reduced to a turbulent—and therefore non-power producing—mass.

If at any point up and down the vertical, that gap becomes wider than the optimum, then at that point the two sails operate independently. The flow leaving the sail in front is reduced in speed, so the second sail has to virtually start again from scratch; the flow from the forward sail is not turned sufficiently towards its after partner to direct it around the camber on the lee side of the second sail as in (fig 1-20(a) and (b)).

Unless the power producing depth of camber is flattened on the aft sail, the flow over the lee surface will be neither strong enough, nor in a sufficiently favourable direction, to resist breaking up into turbulence, and consequently drag.

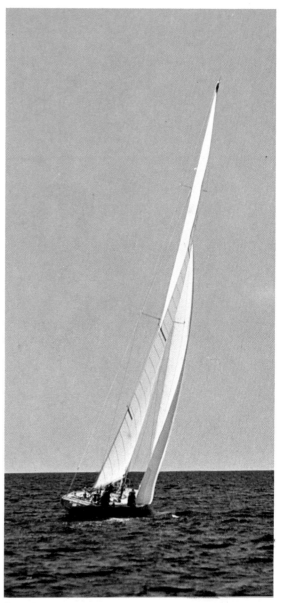

fig 1-22

23

2 Design

The sailmaker's problems begin and end with stretch. How simple it would be to build the perfect sail out of stable material, confident in the knowledge that it would deflect the wind and provide power exactly according to the design criteria—for ever and ever. And to the sailmaker, if such a thing was possible, for example, in thin aluminium sheet, what a wonderful source of income it would prove to be. Every boat would have to have scores of them; one for every five degrees of sailing and a different set for each five extra knots of wind. To say nothing of where this cathedral of tin plate would be stowed.

Of course the whole prospect is too silly for words; but it does attempt to highlight the amazing versatility that we have all come to expect from a modern suit of sails—and the problems facing every sail designer.

Let's just look at these for a moment and for the purpose take the case of a competitive dinghy mainsail. First and foremost it has to produce power, not in one situation, but in a hundred. The shape built into it has to stand up to anything from one to thirty knots of wind. It has to be flat on the wind and fat when running. The sail will spend a good part of its working life flogging aimlessly in the breeze—hardly the perfect treatment for cloth. It is continually soaked, with liberal helpings of salt water from time to time, yet it must weigh next to nothing and never distort. And all of this year in, year out.

Now that would be an impossible dream if it were not for the miracle material polyethylene tetraphthalate. Without it, sailing today would be a very different proposition. For those interested, it is a polymer derived from oil and is known in each country by a trade name which has become part of the language. In America it is Dacron; Terylene in Britain, Tergal in France, Trevira and Diolin in Germany, Tetoron in Japan, Terital in Italy and Terlenka in Holland.

Virtually all fore and aft sails, made today, that is excluding spinnakers, are made from this polyester because, for sailmaking it has some unique properties. Unlike natural fibres, which can be unpredictable, this synthetic material is totally consistent. Its strength and stability are unaffected by moisture. But most important after the weaving process, when heat is applied to the cloth, polyester yarns change shape permanently from long and thin (fig 2-1) to short and fat (fig 2-2). This unique property allows infinitely lighter and more dimensionably stable cloth to be produced than from any other known fibre. The polymer begins life being extruded into strong, hard and dimensionally stable filaments which are then twisted together to form a yarn. It is at this point that the sail designer enters the picture.

It will become obvious as we progress that the finished product on the boat is the sum of a number of design criteria, reaching right back to the basic filament. As the demands of sailors for

fig 2-1

fig 2-2

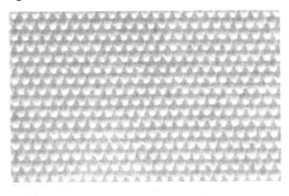

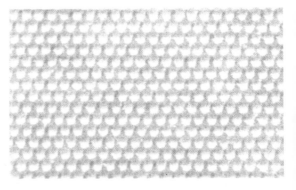

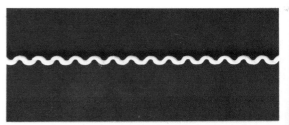

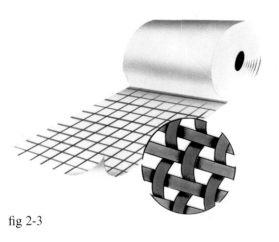

fig 2-3

Yarns

To get back to the yarn. Today's sail designer specifies two yarns for each cloth (fig 2-3); one for the warp (red) and one for the weft (blue). For sailors an easy way to remember the difference is to think of warps as the long 'ropes' that run the length of the cloth panels.

During the weaving process, these warps are stretched horizontally side by side on the loom, alternate yarns separated by a system of frames (fig 2–4). During each weave the frames pull the alternate warps vertically apart. Through this space the wooden bullet-shaped shuttle carrying the weft yarn, which shoots back and forth at high speed, can be seen emerging. The weft is then held straight under tension whilst the warp-holding frames change places wrapping—or crimping— the warps over and under the weft yarns.

The importance of this weft/warp relationship becomes very apparent when we delve a little more

more performance have increased so each sail-maker to a lesser or greater extent has had to retrace his understanding back through the processes. In the early days of polyester, the quantities of cloth used by the boating industry did not warrant research and development programmes by weavers. Only in America was there any real work done, resulting in a lead in sail cloth design and weaving that has since been eroded but not eliminated. Since those days of the early sixties, lofts in most parts of the world have largely caught up and either persuaded weavers and finishers to produce to their own exacting specification, or in a few cases they have gone into production for themselves. The result is that the whole business of cloth design and manufacture is now on a sound technical base, resulting in very little difference between qualities wherever they are produced.

fig 2-4

fig 2-5

fig 2-6

deeply into the question of stretch. To any sort of engineer, stretch presents serious problems whatever the material. To a sailmaker working in fabric and rope it could become a nightmare, unless of course he was able to go right back to square one and specify cloth woven with the exact stretch characteristics required. This is exactly what the designer does; he harnesses the stretch characteristics of his materials to achieve his own ends. What could be an enemy becomes one of the main weapons in his design armoury.

Basically it works like this. Take a piece of woven fabric—a handkerchief is ideal. Pull it first from side to side (fig 2-5). The degree of stretch depends directly on the resistance of the yarns between your hands and on their ability to straighten out under tension. They do this by distorting the yarns woven under and over them. Under the same

tension, stronger (i.e. thicker and straighter yarns of the same material) will stretch less.

Now take hold of the diagonally opposite corners and pull apart (fig 2-6). Immediately the cloth along the diagonal stretches easily, drawing the other two corners toward the line of pull. The little squares made by the criss-crossing weft and warp have now become little diamonds. This bias stretch—again controlled by the relationship between weft and warp and the tightness of the weave, is the built-in adjustment factor of all sails.

Finish

Before examining how these controllable stretch factors are harnessed by the designer, let us round off the sail cloth making process, with the resinating and coating of the cloth; the heat setting and the calendering.

Good sails depend for their shape, particularly from medium winds upwards on the inherent strength and tightness of the weave. However, for some sails, particularly for dinghies, where shape has to be built in, a more structural stiff cloth is beneficial. This extra body is the result of resination where the fabric absorbs a melamine formaldehyde based emulsion which is then cured to give a durable plastic finish to the fabric (fig 2–7).

fig 2-8

Although resination has become progressively more acceptable for yacht sails, and makes a new sail look good, it is in no way a substitute for a well designed tightly woven cloth.

This real strength is developed during the previously mentioned heat-setting process (fig 2-8). As the cloth is heated through a system of rollers, so the yarns change their shape irreversibly by as much as 15 per cent, locking themselves around each other and thereby stabilizing the weave (figs 2-1 and 2-2). Finally the cloth is passed through a further series of heated rollers under considerable

fig 2-7

pressure during what is called calendering. This further enhances the mechanical stability of the cloth and provides it with a smooth surface. There is one other treatment reserved for a certain range of very high performance sails requiring an extremely hard finish. Coating is applied to the cloth after it has been finished, using either epoxide or polyurethane resins.

From this point in the story it becomes increasingly difficult to generalize. Remember, while we have been talking about principles, the designer has been specifying a whole range of quite different cloths each intended for a particular use.

Weft and warp

Before examining how the designer transforms his rolls of flat cloth into stable three-dimensional shapes let us return for a moment to the all important relationship between weft and warp within the cloth.

The weft yarns running across the panel of cloth are the straight ones—or at least the straighter of the two. The exact relationship in each weave remaining the designer's secret.

It is a vivid demonstration of the increase in the designers' influence over the whole sailmakers art to remember that prior to this century no one concerned themselves with whether cloth stretched more one way or another. It was only demands from the competitive sailors of the 1910s led by King Edward VII that pointed Ratsey and Lapthorn of Cowes to make the dramatic breakthrough of the cross-cut sail. Until then sails were scotch-cut i.e. the panels lay parallel with the leech so that there were no weak seams across the points of highest loading (fig 2-9(a)). Ratsey's breakthrough came when they realised that the weft yarn stretch was much more predictable than that of the warps, and so laid their panels at ninety degrees to the leech; lining up the stable weft yarns between head and clew of the sail (fig 2-9(b)).

fig 2-9(a)

fig 2-9(b)

31

fig 2-10

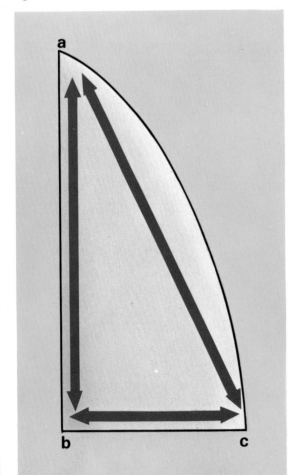

fig 2-11

Mainsail design

That is still the basis of sail design to this day. Let us look then at how the designers first draw their outline mainsail on the loft floor and then fill it with cloth.

Fram
P.O. Box 527
Newburyport, Mass. 01950

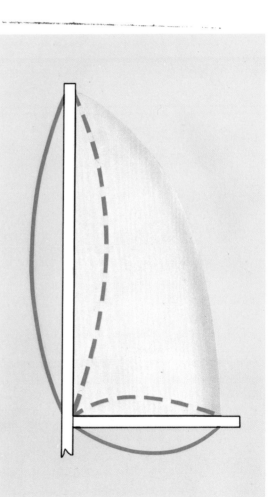

A mainsail (fig 2-10) is supported at three points; Head (a), tack (b) and clew(c). Until the 1960s it is fair to say it was also supported along two sides—the luff and the foot—by the spars. This is no longer true however. Only the mast gives a degree of load support, the boom merely providing a method of adjusting the distance between tack and clew. This largely misunderstood system of foot control is the result of a dramatic change in mainsail design in recent years and we will be amplifying on it later. Suffice at this point to say that the shape of the foot has to be cut to allow the camber to be maintained as low as possible in the sail (fig 2-11).

The designer cuts the luff and foot with a curve of excess cloth (fig 2–12), solid red line, which when set on the straight mast and boom falls back into the sail (broken line). This effect can then be helped by tapering each seam. The important point to remember at this stage is that the cloth meets both foot and luff on the bias, which provides the means as we shall see in the next two chapters to control the shape of the total sail (fig 2-13). The weft yarns (blue) running directly between head and clew provide the necessary resistance to stretch to control the unsupported leech.

fig 2-12

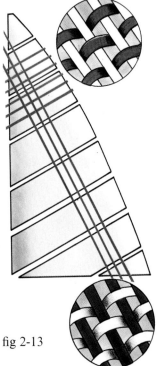

fig 2-13

Traditionally because of cloth limitations it was necessary to provide support for the mainsail foot all along the boom. For the headsail this support was provided by introducing the same principle along the foot of the sail as was applied down the leech (fig 2-15). The relatively stable weft yarns (blue) were lined up along both edges, meeting in a diagonal seam across the centre of the sail; the mitre line.

However, the cloth panels met this mitre line on the bias, and for a given load cloth along the bias has quite different stretch characteristics to that across the foot and leech. We shall examine the

fig 2-14

Headsail design

Now let us turn to headsails. Whereas the main has the rigid support of a mast with which the precise shape of the luff can be controlled, the headsail is dependent for its support solely on the forestay. Under load from the sail the forestay will sag allowing cloth to move back into the body of the sail (fig 2-14). To counteract this the designer has to introduce a concave curve to his headsail luff (inset).

The dramatic breakthroughs in cloth technology which have revolutionized mainsail design have also had their effect on headsails.

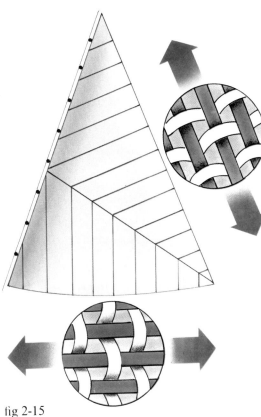

fig 2-15

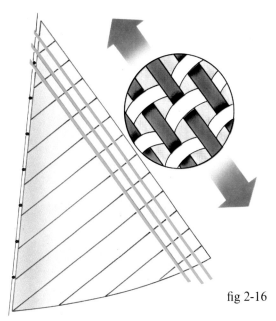

fig 2-16

yacht sails were tried. Today, thanks to better and better cloth, virtually all performance headsails are cross-cut (fig 2–17).

problems of balancing these when we look at headsails in detail.

The alternative headsail design, which emerged in the 70s, uses exactly the same principle as that of the modern mainsail. The leech of the sail has the weft yarn to support it (fig 2-16), and the cloth is sufficiently stable to allow control throughout the body of the sail to be achieved from a single point—the clew.

Dinghies, with their relatively low loadings, were the first to use this cross-cut system for their headsails; but it was not long before light weather

fig 2-17

3 The main-sail

To the sailmaker there are two types of boats. Those exactly the same as boats he has made sails for before and those that are not.

It so happens that most in the first category are one-designs and production boats complying with strict class rules; the others are cruisers and rated boats, which tend to be more individual in both design and dimension.

However, this is coincidental.

Whether it be for dinghy or cruiser, if the sailmaker's past experience includes enough sails for that type, the chances are that patterns exist for each panel of the sail, and that they will be subject to continual refinements, revisions and updating. That will be as true for a production ocean racer, as it is for a 470 centreboarder.

However, if the sail is for a one-off boat, or an unfamiliar dinghy, then the sailmaker has to resort to a system of design.

To meet these infinitely variable demands, the more sophisticated sailmakers today have programmed computers to do the job. Do not be misled however into thinking this has transformed the design of a sail into a soulless operation; far from it.

Any investment in continual improvement of the system more than makes up for the time saved on purely mathematical problems.

Whether the sailmaker uses a computer, or sheets and sheets of paper covered in numerical scrawl, the result is the same; a series of off-sets to which the sail will be cut. These are translated on the cutting floor, via long flexible battens (fig 3-1) bent around prickers, to produce a chalk outline.

fig 3-1

37

The majority of sails made for non-displacement type boats i.e. dinghies, are made from panels for which individual patterns exist (fig 3-2).

In this way the sailmaker is able to reproduce for his everyday customer, exactly the same sail that he cut for a world champion.

This ability to duplicate a successful shape is more critical to dinghy sails than it is to those for larger boats. Dinghy sails benefit from being made from firmer and therefore less elastic cloth. Primarily this is because the boat and rig are themselves less stable in the water and their sails are subject to continuous fluctuations as they bounce along over the waves (fig 3-3). It is important also that they are able to cope with a wider range of conditions than yacht sails, without constant adjustment:

fig 3-2

fig 3-3

38

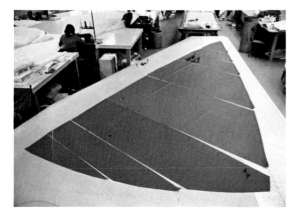

allowing the crew to concentrate on sailing the boat. All of these factors are reflected in the number of sets of patterns held by the sailmaker for a single sail.

It is not unusual for a performance sailmaker to have six different patterns for one class of dinghy mainsail all related to both crew weight, whether the boat will be sailed inland or on the sea, and the range of wind strengths likely to be encountered.

Series production sails like these are cut, panel by panel from the appropriate pattern and laid out side by side on a sailmaking table (fig 3-4) or on the loft floor. Pencil marks are made along the edge of each panel to serve as registers for when they are sewn together.

The one-off sail, for which no patterns have been developed, will have its chalk outline, drawn on the loft floor, filled panel by panel from a roll of cloth (fig 3-5).

Once all the panels are cut to shape they are passed to a machinist who will sew them together, usually

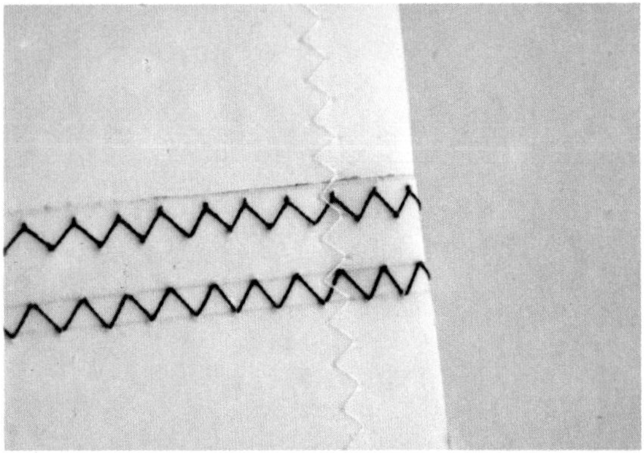

fig 3-6

using a thread of contrasting colour (fig 3-6). This apparently minor point fulfils two important functions. It allows the sailmaker, and later the sailor, to see if any threads are broken or frayed; vital with polyester sails as the cloth is so unyielding that the stitches will always remain proud and

therefore exposed to chafe. Secondly, a contrasting colour along each seam allows the sailor to read his sail shape once it is up and drawing.

On a big mainsail or genoa, the machinist feeds the panels towards the needles from a roll, balanced on her shoulder (fig 3–7), in order that she can see and therefore stitch each seam accurately.

Once the sail has been seamed it goes back to the table or floor for the next stage, usually referred to as spreading. Multiple layers of cloth are prepared for head, tack and clew corners, and any other areas, such as around reefing points and cringles which will be subject to extra strain. These will be added before the cringles are hand sewn—or these days much more commonly swaged (fig 3-8) into the corners, and the headboard fitted.

The doubling hem around the roach of the mainsail is known as the tabling. Its sole purpose is

fig 3-7

to prevent the leech fraying, but because it means that the thickness of the tabling will not stretch, under tension, at the same rate as the adjacent single cloth of the sail, it is worthy of a little explanation.

At the cutting stage an over large margin of cloth is left along the roach outline. Were this margin to be simply turned in towards the centre of the sail and then sewn down (fig 3-9(a)), two problems would arise. Under load the leech will hook as the double thickness tabling stretches less than the rest of the leech area. Secondly, to accommodate the curve of the roach, when the margin is turned over the weft and warp threads will not align with those in the body of the sail. Under load this will produce unequal stretch properties within the tabling itself.

The answer is to cut off the tabling strip (fig 3-10) leaving the sail just marginally larger. This tiny margin is turned over and the tabling strip reapplied over the raw edge (fig 3-9 (b)). This overcomes the second problem; the yarns of the table now align perfectly with those along the roach.

fig 3-8

fig 3-9

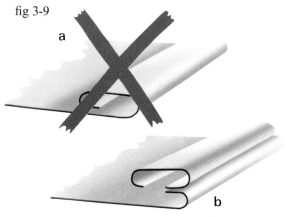

fig 3-10

The first and more important problem is solved by slightly gathering the tabling whilst it is attached to the tensioned leech. In this way the edge of the sail is allowed to stretch a little before the doubled tabling comes under load. On small dinghy-type mainsails a strip of cloth is simply folded over the edge of the leech, and then stitched through the sail. Or the leech can be cut using a hot-knife which seals the weave. This latter makes for a more fragile edge and is consequently more popular with sailors to whom performance matters more than long life.

The final major operation is to marry the sail to its luff and foot tapes or ropes. We mention both as this will depend on the type of spars with which the boat is equipped and on your sailmaker's practice.

Nowadays most good mainsails depend for their stretch control characteristics on a specially woven

fig 3-11

married to their tapes at relatively low loadings. They are usually held firm with prickers along each edge, whilst the tapes are applied (fig 3-12). Virtually all dinghy, and many yacht spars, are equipped with integral grooves designed to take bolt ropes. These ropes should not be confused with the old-fashioned luff and foot rope which was sewn directly to the sail. Modern luff tapes contain a rope (fig 3-13), but it is independent of the actual sail and purely there to hold the sail in the spar groove and/or to restrict over-enthusiastic application of the halyard winch on a yacht.

What are the advantages of either sliders or a bolt rope for attaching a mainsail to mast and boom? Certainly a rope to run along the boom groove appears to be best. It seals the join very well. Sliders tend to cause vertical drawmarks along the sail, when the outhaul is slackened off to encourage a full foot, thus spoiling the flow.

fig 3-12

luff tape, which is quicker and easier to fit and which controls stretch more accurately than the traditionally hand-sewn bolt-rope. Of course this tape is more substantial than the sail cloth to which it is attached. Just as with the tabling it is therefore necessary to stretch out the sail before marrying the two together. In this way tape and sail will be matched and balanced when the sail comes under load.

In the case a yacht sail this operation is carried out between three strong points in the loft (fig 3-11). For the first time the sail takes on its designed shape.

Mainsails for light boats, such as racing dinghies, not being subjected to such high forces in use, are

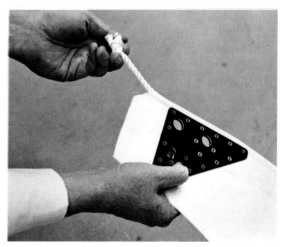

fig 3-13

On the other hand, sliders are preferable for the mast, particularly if you are sailing short-handed—and what cruising man isn't. With sliders, when you lower the sail, it stays attached to the mast, ready to hoist again by simply hauling on the halyard. With the bolt rope and groove this is impossible; as any dinghy sailor will testify; the whole sail comes flying down all over the place and has to be collected up for stowing—hopefully before it goes over the side. O.K. for the heavily crewed racing yacht but otherwise more trouble than it is worth. Whether there is any great aerodynamic advantage to a seal between mast and mainsail is doubtful—the whole area directly behind the spar being a mass of turbulence anyway.

Trim

When the dimensions of a yacht mainsail are given to the sailmaker, they should correspond with the maximum distances between the tack and the limiting points on the mast and boom, to which the halyard and outhaul can pull the sail (fig 3-14). The foot length should be taken from the aft edge of the mast, not from the tack-pin, although the sailmaker will want to know the distance between the mast and the tack-pin so that he can give the tack and lower part of the luff the correct shape.

The three positions mentioned are marked with black bands on many racing boats. If yours is not, there are almost certainly other restrictions which govern sail size such as class rules and non-adjustable halyards.

A modern performance mainsail is made to

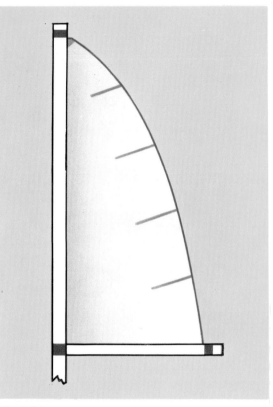

fig 3-14

perform well to windward in medium weather when set to these limits.

Let us make a start on mainsail trim. Set the boat up on the wind in 10–15 knots of apparent wind with the luff to its marks; the outhaul almost at its limit, and the mainsheet just tight enough to stop the luff lifting.

Now look carefully at the seams in the upper half of the sail (fig 3-15). This yacht sail has a coloured strip of cloth sewn across the chord, but that is simply a racing luxury. The seams give you exactly the same information.

Here you can see that the deepest part of the sail is around half way between luff and leech. That is where it should remain in the mainsail at all times. The only exception is when the mainsail is the only sail—the cat-rig—where it should be between a half and one third back from the luff.

You will notice that the lower seams appear to be flatter. This is purely an optical illusion— accentuated admittedly in this case by the camera. The human eye however plays the same trick. Seams at eye level appear to be dead straight. It is

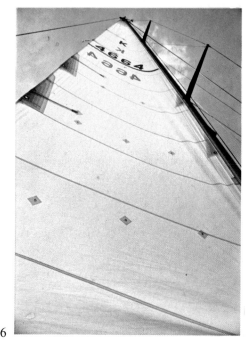

fig 3-16

fig 3-15

important therefore to pick a point fairly high up on the sail for reference.

Now let us look at the controls with which you can alter this shape, and first at the control of luff tension.

On this Three-quarter Ton class the luff was over-tensioned by a mere 10 cm (fig 3-16). The maximum point of flow has moved forward and vertical stretch lines have appeared along the luff. The bias stretch of the panels at the luff, turning from squares to upright diamonds has pulled all the flow towards the mast.

What is not so obvious is that this has set up a chain reaction right along each panel, which has relaxed the tension on the leech, allowing it to fall off to leeward.

Exactly the opposite happens if you slack off the halyard past its optimum point, or allow the tack end of the boom on those boats with sliding goosenecks to rise too far. The flow moves back into the aft half of the sail. The luff entry flattens in even a modest wind, and the leech tightens up again to windward.

Now it is all very well talking about adjusting the luff tension but what about the sailor whose halyard is cleated or hooked off at one position— maximum hoist. How can he adjust his flow by luff tension? The answer is by a Cunningham hole. This is simply a second cringle or sheave positioned above the tack at a distance equal to the designed maximum stretch of that particular sail's luff (fig 3-17). A line leading from the base of the mast is usually passed through the sail at this point and cleated or jammed off down on the other side of the mast. This gives a simple two-to-one purchase and allows tension to be adjusted quickly and conveniently. Tension, applied at the bottom of the luff via this control-line, works exactly the same way as if it came via the halyard (fig 3-18). Indeed it has one advantage over the halyard. Using a Cunningham, the luff tension can be adjusted without slackening the main sheet.

The evolution of the Cunningham was however based on a simple premise. It allowed the sail to be cut to its maximum dimensions for light airs.

All we have attempted so far is to utilize the sail's

fig 3-17

fig 3-18

built-in cloth mechanics to control the position of the flow by altering luff tension. We have not as yet attempted to control the amount of flow. This is the separate and very different function of the clew outhaul, and in the case of some racing boats the clew Cunningham.

In order to understand how best to operate the mainsail controls, consider first the true function of the boom. In the last chapter we emphasized that the mainsail foot had no functional support from the boom, except at the clew. The boom exists only to give precise three-dimensional control of the clew position—upwards and downwards, side to side, and backwards and forwards. The fact that the foot of the mainsail is usually connected to the boom by a shelf of cloth is more convention than function. Some maintain that this shelf steers the wind across the sail rather than letting it spill away underneath—the 'end-plate' effect. But there is a growing number of devotees of the loose-footed mainsail, which allows the body of the sail to hang below the level of the boom, gaining some extra area. The important thing to remember from now on is that the method of controlling a loose-footed and shelf-footed mainsail is identical.

The existence or shape of the shelf is of little consequence and therefore the effect of adjusting the foot tension is totally different from that of adjusting luff tension.

This brings us to the clew outhaul with which we control precisely the distance between the clew and the tack (fig 3-19). Easing the clew outhaul

fig 3-19

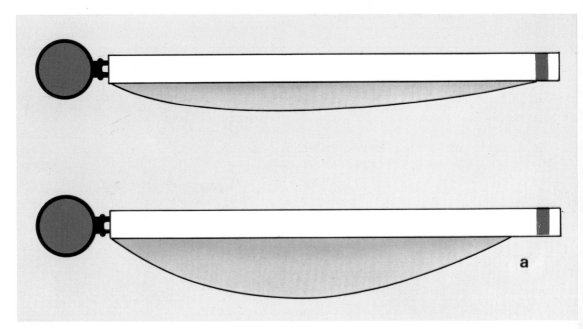

fig 3-20   fig 3-21   fig 3-22

forward (a) (without adjusting the mainsheet) will not only bring the clew closer to the tack. It will bring it closer to any point on the mast from top to bottom, adding greater depth of camber throughout the whole height of the sail.

The three pairs of pictures (fig 3-20/21/22) show how relatively small differences in the amount of outhaul tension affect the depth of camber in a shelf-footed mainsail. It is not greatly noticeable when viewed from aft although the clew position is clearly seen. However, the difference is dramatic when seen from before the mast. Notice in particular how in each of the three positions, as the outhaul is eased, the sail becomes fuller, *but* the

49

boom remains at the same angle with the centre line.

An extension of the range of control possible with the clew outhaul is the clew Cunningham. It corresponds with the luff Cunningham being placed on the leech at a point above the clew (fig 3-

fig 3-23

23). In order that additional tension can be applied along the foot of the sail, while still not extending it beyond the black band limit, it is necessary to provide an acute angle of pull, between the Cunningham and the boom. This is why a long, thin wedge of cloth is added to the foot, causing the boom to droop at its outer end. If it is necessary to flatten the sail further, once the clew has reached its limit, a second outhaul between the clew Cunningham and the boom end is tightened, lifting the boom to the horizontal and at the same time tensioning the foot (fig 3-24).

fig 3-24

This action further flattens the camber in the sail (fig 3-25), compared with that allowed by the clew at its black band limit (fig 3-22).

Let us now consider the control provided by mainsheet traveller and vang (or kicking strap).

If the mainsheet traveller had the same sweeping length of arc as the boom could swing, it would be easy. We could then say that all the up-and-down adjustment of the boom, controlling mainsail leech tension, could be the role of the mainsheet (fig 3-26(a)). Then all sideways adjustment, controlling the angle at which the sail is presented to the wind, could be the role of the mainsheet traveller (green). But the boat is never wide enough for this arrangement (b), which becomes valid only for windward sailing where the boom is close to the centreline of the boat and within the arc of the traveller. Once outside the arc of the traveller, the vertical load on the clew must be taken by the vang (c) and the mainsheet must take over the role of the traveller in presenting the sail to the wind at the right angle.

fig 3-25

fig.3-26(a) fig.3-26(b) fig.3-26(c)

fig 3-26

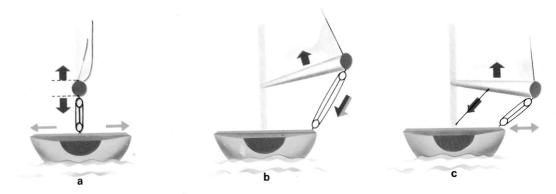

a

b

c

Twist

fig 3-28

The downward load on the clew—whether by vang or mainsheet—controls the tension in the leech of the sail. As this tension is slackened, the upper part of the sail is no longer held up at the same angle to the wind as the boom at the bottom. This creates the effect known as twist (fig 3-27).

We have already seen how important it is to present the sail at its correct angle to the apparent wind direction. This is not as straightforward as it seems. The wind speed is slower close to the surface of the water because of friction, than it is high up.

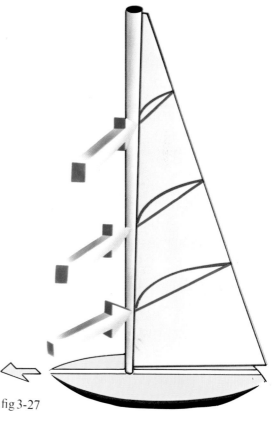

fig 3-27

We can see from our analysis of apparent wind in Chapter 1 that where the true wind is slower, the apparent wind direction is more affected by the speed of the boat than where the true wind is faster. This means that the apparent wind direction close to the water will be from further forward than it appears at the top of the mast (fig 3-28), creating the need for some degree of twist to allow for this variation.

53

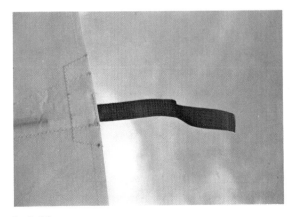

fig 3-29

fig 3-30 (a, b, c)

The wind gradient is at its steepest and most noticeable in light air when the surface friction has a greater relative effect. The degree of twist *allowed to develop* in the mainsail to compensate for this change in apparent wind direction is controlled by the vertical adjustment of the boom via the mainsheet. This is simply achieved by bringing the traveller to windward until the lower part of the sail is presented to the wind at the correct angle. The sheet is then eased to allow the upper leech to twist off.

When the correct trim is achieved, the wind will flow freely off the leech from both windward and leeward surfaces. As an indication of whether this is happening correctly, nothing can beat small strips of coloured nylon (fig 3-29), each about six inches long, sewn to the outer edge of each batten pocket.

In light to medium airs (fig 3-30), bring the traveller to windward until the lowest strip disappears behind the leech to leeward (a). Then ease until the lowest tell-tale streams aft. Transferring one's gaze to the top streamer; if it is out of sight, (b) ease the mainsheet and vang if tensioned, until it also streams happily aft again (c). If it is already streaming (d) tighten the mainsheet until it disappears (e) and slack off just enough to make it stream again (f).

fig 3-30
(d, e, f)

In these same light to medium airs what should we be looking for in the main as sheets are cracked and the boat reaches and then runs?

Aloft the point of deepest draft should remain at the midpoint of the sail. Because the apparent wind speed has inevitably dropped from the beat, this will mean less luff tension. Ease the halyard or

Cunningham until the seams look right. We have already seen the way to make the sail fuller: ease the clew outhaul until the desired depth of camber has been achieved.

Off the wind the clew will be out of the range of the main sheet traveller. Vertical control via the mainsheet will be lost; that job having to be taken over by the boom vang. The conventional vang can either be a simple block purchase, a cam-type lever, a geared roller or, on a yacht, a solid spar with a screw or hydraulic adjuster. It connects a point on the lower side of the boom to the lowest available point on the mast. An alternative is a

figs 3-31 (a, b, c)

fig 3-31(d)

simple purchase between the boom and lee deck or toe-rail. This has the added advantage of preventing that unexpected gybe.

One cannot over-estimate the importance of vertical control over the aft section of the sail. We saw (fig 3-26 (a, b and c)) what happens when the sheet can no longer hold the mainsail leech tight: in (b) the eased mainsheet allowed the boom to rise resulting in excessive twist and loss of power. A satisfactory airfoil was restored in (c) once tension was applied with a vang.

Once the sheets have been eased the biggest problem facing the crew is to know whether the sail is retaining that all important air flow over the lee surface. If the sail is eased too far the luff will flutter. Over sheeted, it will stall and the turbulence formed will immediately upset the flow of the leech tell-tales. If the upper ones disappear (fig 3-31(a)) then the top part of the sail is stalled to leeward. Ease the vang to free the upper leech and gently trim the main sheet to keep the lower strips streaming aft (b). Should only the lower tell-tale(s) disappear (c), the upper half of the sail is twisting off too far and the lower section is stalled. Down with the vang and ease the sheet until all four are streaming out from the sail (d); proof that the airflow is leaving the leeward surface in an even, smooth and power producing manner.

We will be returning to mainsails on both dinghies and yachts in separate chapters to consider what happens when the wind pipes up, and also their interaction with foresails. At that point we will look at how mast bend can be harnessed to provide additional flow control.

However, as we are still off the wind, here perhaps is a good point to introduce a simple device used on yachts to exert a greater degree of control over the mainsail leech.

This is the leech line; a light cord attached to the top of the leech and led down through the tabling, following the curve of the roach (fig 3-32 (a)). It emerges close to the clew and can be led forward along the boom to a small cleat. From here it can be adjusted when the clew itself is out of reach.

fig 3-32

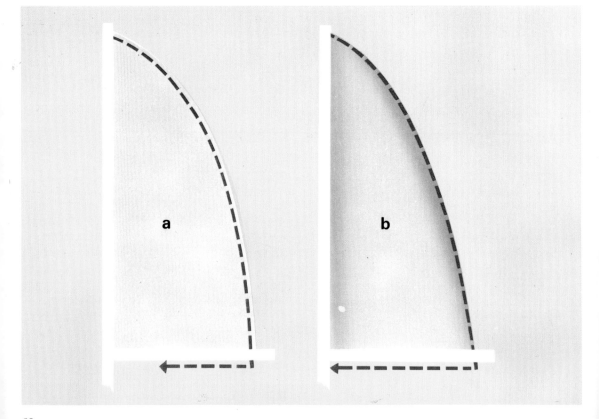

58

fig 3-33

Tensioning on this line will control any tendency
for the leech to flutter (fig 3-32 (b)). Off the wind,
further tension will straighten out the round of the
roach, pulling it forward and to windward (fig
3-33). This deepens the camber along the after
edge of the sail. If this is done, remember to slacken
the line before coming on to the wind and hauling tight on the mainsheet. Otherwise you will
probably break the relatively light leech line.

4 Headsails

The techniques used to make headsails are very similar to those for mainsails. There are however, differences in detail and it is worth looking at these, as well as amplifying on the choice between cross-cut and mitre-cut mentioned earlier.

Why the two types?

We have seen how camber in the sail can be controlled by varying tension across the bias of the weave along the luff. But this distortion under load of the woven squares into elongated diamonds does not just occur along the luff. It happens all over the sail, and particularly near the corners.

Consider what is happening at the clew of the mainsail with the weft yarns running parallel with the leech (fig 4-1).

The weight of wind in the centre of the sail is exerting a high load (red) diagonally down to the clew. As this pull is across the bias, the weave is distorted into diamonds in the opposite direction to those on the luff, drawing the foot and leech closer together (blue arrows). Along the leech this inward collapse is limited, due to the extra stability provided by the parallel weft yarns.

The foot however is solely dependent on the amount of bias stability in the cloth to prevent its upwards collapse.

fig 4-1

This is why, prior to the development of the new sail fabrics, it was necessary for the mainsail to be supported by a boom all the way along the length of the foot.

This too is why old-fashioned mainsails (fig 4-2) were relatively inefficient. The strong vertical pull along the full length of the boom destroyed the camber in the lower part of the sail, wasting much of its area.

Mitres

For the headsail foot, with neither cloth with sufficient bias stability nor a rigid boom to hand, sailmakers had to find an alternative answer. They did this (as briefly mentioned in Chapter 1) by lining up the cloth panels with their weft along the foot as well as the leech (fig 4–3). Where the panels met in the middle of the sail they were joined by a line which bisected the clew: the mitre line.

For the sail to adopt the correct shape in the wind strength for which it was designed, the sailmaker must predict and allow for the amount of collapse

fig 4-2

fig 4-3

that will take place—forward from the leech and upwards from the foot.

If the weft yarns stay parallel to the concave collapse curves on leech and foot throughout their upper and lower respective triangles, the opposite sides of each section will become convex (fig 4-4).

This excess cloth will make the sail very deep and baggy, so the mitre is cut with a concave curve on either side (fig 4-5). This is sufficient to pull the mitre into a straight line once the sail has settled into its mechanical balance under load. A similar adjustment along the luff is taken into account when the sailmaker is calculating the amount of convex curve he will allow to match the anticipated forestay sag when the sail comes under load.

All very straightforward and logical you may say. That is until you remember that the forces on which this critical balance depends are far from constant. The green cross sections (fig 4-5) show what happens. If the wind is too light it will not

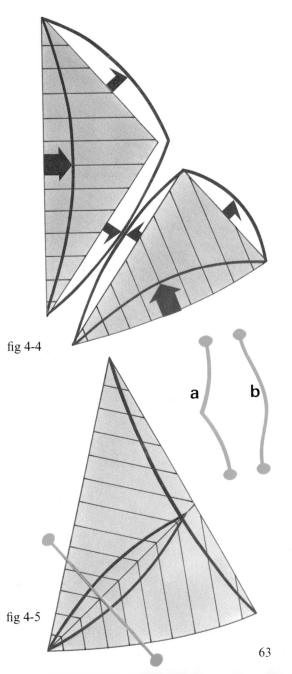

fig 4-4

a b

fig 4-5

63

move enough cloth into the centre of the sail (a) and the mitre will stand hard and proud. Too much wind will cause excessive collapse and the mitre will sag away to leeward (b).

To help overcome this problem the sailmaker retraced his steps to the cloth design stage. The result was the close ratio cloth developed specially for, and used only in mitred headsails.

By specifying a finer weft yarn the difference between stretch across the panel and that along the bias can be minimized. This allows the leech and foot to stretch quite considerably under high loadings, which in turn allows the distance between clew and luff to be increased. Excess camber in the belly of the sail is reduced, and the combination of this tension and that along the luff, smooths out any unevenness at the mitre.

So, we now have a sail, the shape of which can be adequately, if not perfectly, controlled by two direct tensions. Tension along the luff will control the position of greatest flow; whilst tension on the sheet will control the depth.

Cross-cut

The need for constant adjustment to cope with differing wind strengths is a particularly acute problem on dinghies. Fortunately their headsails are subjected to much lower loadings; the boats are more easily driven than displacement boats, and the smaller headsail of the non-masthead rig plays a relatively minor role in the total sail plan.

It was practical therefore, with the cloth available at the time to consider for dinghies at least using a cut similar to that developed for the mainsail which no longer required mechanical support along the boom. This was the beginning of the cross-cut headsail.

Each panel, as with a mainsail, is laid into the triangle with the weft parallel with the leech. Immediately we see that cloth along the leech will have quite different stretch characteristics to that which meets the foot on the bias. Were an equal amount of tension applied along both, as with the mitre-cut, the leech would harden into a flat line and the foot would merely stretch. The depth of camber from the head to the foot of the sail is now dependent on the direct distance between the luff and the clew, whilst vertical tension via the jib sheet gives precise control over the shape of the leech.

As the inherent stability of available cloth improved, sailmakers began, cautiously at first, to experiment with cross-cut headsails for larger yachts. By the mid 1970s cloth design and weaving techniques had been developed to the point where the cross-cut became a practical proposition for the maximum size genoas needed for lighter conditions (fig 4-6).

It is in these conditions that the benefits of the cross-cut over the mitre-cut are most apparent. Full size genoas have to perform under a wider range of loadings than any other headsail: from a zephyr when the sheet can be hand held, to their top limit when a man uses all his strength on a powerful winch to haul the sail in. It is impossible to perfect the intricate mechanics of the mitred headsail throughout this wide range. Heavier weather sails present less of a problem as their working wind range is always narrower, although

fig 4-6

fig 4-7
fig 4-7

with better and better cloths it is now possible to make cross-cut heavy weather genoas and jibs (fig 4-7). These have led directly to the development of a headsail which can be reefed.

For the cross-cut sail, where the sailmaker has to place all his faith in cloth stability to prevent foot collapse, he has been forced to use a cloth with a very firm and hard finish. Mitred sails on the other hand are best made from soft and more mobile cloth.

This difference in cloth gives each type an advantage over the other for both cruising and racing yachtsmen.

On the one hand the cruising man will prefer the softer mitred sail as it can be more easily stuffed into a small bag which will take up less space below deck. The stiffer cross-cut sails should best be folded before packing and by necessity need a larger bag or a turtle. Sail storage space becomes a major factor when laying out the interior of a racing yacht (fig 4-8).

On the other hand the springy weft needed for the mitred sail construction creates a degree of leech and foot stretch which makes constant sheet adjustment imperative, if optimum performance is to be achieved. A considerable disadvantage to the short handed cruising man.

Once it is set correctly, the firmer cloth of the cross-cut will withstand fluctuation in wind strength with very little adjustment.

Finally, before leaving the mitre versus the cross-cut debate, it is worth mentioning that the latter cannot be used for sails with a markedly obtuse clew, such as a high clew yankee (fig 4-9). The cross-cut is impracticable here due to the angle at which the panels meet the foot.

Much of what we have already said about flow control in mainsails applies equally to headsails. Let us therefore concentrate on the points where they differ.

fig 4-8

fig 4-9

fig 4-10

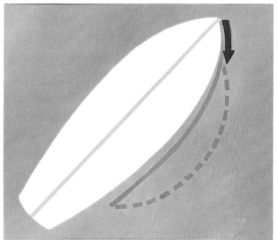

Luff

Under load from the sail the flexible stay which supports the luff of a headsail will sag. It is practically impossible to eliminate this sag entirely, although there are a number of ways that it can be minimized. We discuss mast and rig tune in detail later, but it is important to stress here the vital need for adequate support of the headsail luff if performance, particularly to windward, is to be achieved.

As the loads induced by the wind increase (fig 4-10), relative to the tension exerted between the

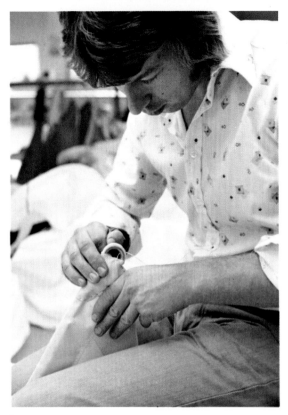

fig 4-11

points at either end of the forestay, so cloth is dropped back into the sail (red arrow). This is the opposite of what is wanted. The sail becomes fuller (dotted line) in the increased wind, rather than flatter.

To minimize the sag, wire, or on some yachts stainless steel rod, has to be used to give the necessary luff support. Whether this is an integral part of the sail, or exists as a standing part of the rig, depends on the type of boat. These days the need for a wire forestay *and* a wire luff-rope has virtually disappeared. Few dinghy jibs are still equipped with hanks to attach them to a forestay. In many cases the forestay itself has disappeared.

Its primary function, that of giving forward support for the mast, is taken over by a wire running up inside a sleeve in the sail itself. This wire also provides luff support. Because of the rigidity of dinghy jib fabric, and the relatively low loadings encountered, constant adjustment of flow position is unnecessary. The head and tack of the sail may be permanently seized at the optimum tension to the swaged eyes at either end of this luff wire (fig 4-11). Alternatively, the one end of the sail, usually the head, may be fitted with a lanyard allowing limited adjustment of sail luff tension relative to that of the wire.

On larger boats equipped with standing wire or rod headstays, luff wires have been made largely redundant by advances in cloth design.

Wire, which once allowed the tension along the bias of the luff to be pre-judged and fixed to cope with a given narrow band of windspeed would today simply limit the sail's versatility. Only on storm jibs are luff wires widely used—and then it is for safety. The luff wire allows them to be set flying if any of the gear which attaches sail to forestay, or indeed the forestay itself, should break.

Virtually all yacht headsails are now equipped with stretchy luffs: woven tapes and/or ropes similar to those used on mainsails. These allow the necessary stretch along the bias with which the position of camber can be adjusted for a wide range of wind speeds.

Whether the luff has a wire, rope or tape, the best method of attaching sail to forestay for the cruising man is with the traditional hank (fig 4-12). When the sail is lowered it remains, along the luff at least, attached firmly to the vessel. We shall look at the various 'headfoil' systems in chapter six. Suffice to say here that the luff tapes developed to slide up inside the foils are similar in concept to the bolt ropes used to hold the mainsail luff into the mast groove.

fig 4-12

fig 4-13

Leech

Turning to the leech, the sailmaker is faced with something of a dilemma. On the one hand he wants a smooth exhaust for the accelerated flow, which, if the rest of the sail has done its job properly, should be of equal pressure on either surface of the sail by the time it reaches the leech. On the other hand this equalized pressure would cause the leech to flutter: and nothing can be more annoying and distracting to helmsman and crew alike, than a flapping leech.

For maximum size headsails, usually cut with a straight leech, he solves the problem by positioning flow in the optimum position so that the leech will flutter, and then fitting that leech with a light line inside the tabling—similar to that around the roach of a mainsail. The crew can then damp down any tendency to flutter by increasing the tension

fig 4-14

on this leech line. As conditions vary, it should be constantly adjusted (fig 4-13) so that the leech is just not quite on the point of flutter.

For heavy weather sails, where maximum area is unimportant, the part which would want to flutter is cut away, making the leech curve hollow.

Foot

One role of the shelf along the foot of a modern mainsail is to steer across the sail, wind, which might otherwise escape below. This 'end plate' effect becomes even more significant on headsails where it is possible to block the gap between the sail and the deck (fig 4-14) by deepening the foot roach and dropping the clew.

Changes in the offshore rules governing yachts, now make it advantageous to raise the clew a little higher, but a deeper foot roach allows the seal along the front half of the foot length at least to be maintained. The need to obtain all available power does not apply with heavy weather headsails. They are best cut without much foot round to allow any water coming over the bow to escape freely.

In the dinghy and smaller racing boat classes the end plate effect has been sought with equal enthusiasm. Even to the point in some sails where luff length has been sacrificed in order to lower the clew.

On small boats there is a further factor which has led to the development of the 'aerofoil foot' (fig 4-15).

fig 4-15

71

The force exerted on a relatively small sail via the sheet by the crew sitting out or trapezing to windward is quite liable to pull all of the camber out of a dinghy jib, destroying its drive. The flat cloth of the aerofoil foot plays a similar role to that of the mainsail boom controlling the distance between the clew and tack, but using fabric rather than a rigid strut. Not only is the camber retained. The shaping along the foot also provides a marked degree of control over its position, within the sail.

fig 4-16

Trim

After this analysis of the physical features of headsails, let us put these sails to work.

The principles of flow control for headsails are the same as those applying to mainsails. However, because the headsail is limited by a single diagonal pull at the clew, flow control is much harder to break down into specific elements.

For instance in sails with adjustable luffs, the position of maximum camber in varying winds can be controlled with luff tension. But easing the sheet to sail more freely will reduce the load on the sail. To balance the tensions within the sail the luff must be eased simultaneously—and vice versa.

The position of maximum camber should not therefore be adjusted until the sail is sheeted in correctly. This in itself demands halyard winches powerful enough to stretch the sail under its full load.

When correctly trimmed the maximum depth of flow in any headsail on any point of sailing should be between one third and half way back from the luff (fig 4-16). On sails with wire luffs and those made from harder finished cloths, the retention of this position will depend largely on the stability of the fabric. In sails made from more mobile cloth, the precise position can be adjusted by luff tension.

Tightening the luff, either via the halyard, or a Cunningham hole, will drag flow forward (fig 4-17). This is by no means as detrimental to performance as having the luff too slack. In (fig 4-18) due to insufficient luff tension, the maximum flow has been forced into the after part of the sail. Pressure is now building up on the windward surface of the leech, and flow can no longer exhaust smoothly onto the leeward surface of the mainsail.

The correct position of maximum flow is therefore critical. But equally that flow must be uniformly distributed up and down the whole height of the sail. This will depend on the correct sheeting angle.

fig 4-17

fig 4-18

Sheeting position

In the case of small non-masthead rigged boats such as the modern high performance dinghy a further complication enters the picture. Because of size of the jib relative to the more important mainsail, fairlead position is largely used to control the jib leech into a curve parallel to the leeward surface of the mainsail. This technique is dealt with in the next chapter, so while the following sheet lead principles apply to all headsails, perhaps we should here emphasize their relevance to masthead rigs where the headsail is the more important in producing drive.

On boats where the fore and aft position of the sheet fairlead can be adjusted, we find the correct position for each sail using a 'guess it—test it' system.

The first stage—guess it—depends on the cut of the sail. For the cross-cut (fig 4-19) the rule is that the projected line of the sheet (red) through the clew should meet the luff of the sail at its mid point. This line does not bisect the clew angle, but is always very much steeper. In the case of either the mitred sail (fig 4-20), with its line of load-taking weft along the foot, or a sail with an 'aerofoil' foot, the sheet lead (blue line) must be brought further aft to counteract the effect of this restraint.

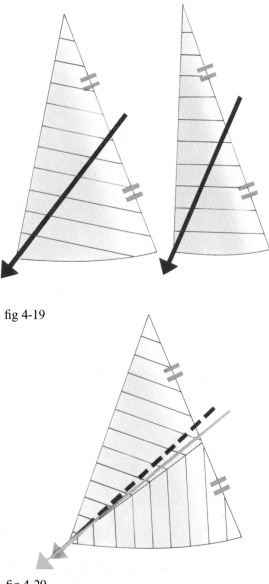

fig 4-19

fig 4-20

fig 4-21

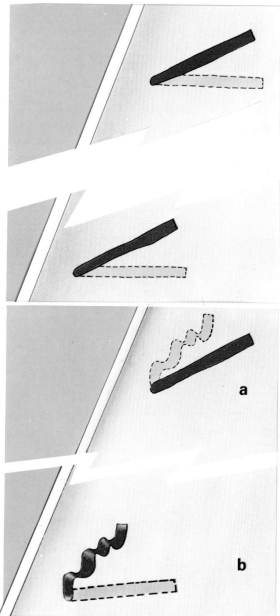

For the 'test it' stage, we rely on our humble little friends, the tell-tales. How any racing sailor can afford to be without these simple aids is hard to understand. Headsail tell-tales are short lengths of light nylon ribbon or wool placed close to the luff at regular intervals (fig 4-21). In this position they tell the sailor what is happening as the flow is deflected over either side of the headsail.

Whilst stick-on versions are commercially available, by far the easiest and cheapest method is to pass a length of dark wool through the sail fabric, using a darning needle, and fixing it in position with an overhand knot on either side. They should all be the same distance from the luff; between six and twelve inches depending on the size of the sail.

If the sail is sheeted in too tightly, the tell-tales on the leeward side will lift and dance (fig 4-22(a)) in the turbulence caused by the breaking up airflow. If the sail is not sheeted in sufficiently, then those on the windward side will behave in a similar manner (b).

Equally, by telling us that flow is not uniformly distributed between the top and bottom of the sail, the tell-tales can lead us to the precise sheet fairlead position.

fig 4-22

With the sail sheeted in hard, luff the boat slowly into the wind. If the lower windward tell-tales lift and dance before those at the top, then the sail is under-sheeted at the bottom. More backward pull is needed by the sheet, so move the fairlead aft. If the tell-tales at the top dance first then the fairlead has to be moved forward, until they all move in unison. The same principle applies, whatever the cut of the headsail.

Of course the primary role of luff tell-tales is to let helmsman and crew see the wind whilst sailing—and particularly when sailing to windward. Off the wind they enable the crew accurately to present the fore part of the sail directly into the wind (fig 4-23). With the sails sheeted in hard when sailing to windward, they allow the helmsman to keep the boat at a constant angle to the fluctuating wind for optimum performance. That angle incidently is when all windward tell-tales are just on the point of lifting.

Tension by Cunningham

Having used the tell-tales to find the correct sheet fairlead position, the point of maximum flow can, as we have already mentioned, be adjusted by altering tension in the luff of the sail. Whilst this is commonly achieved via the halyard, there are advantages to be gained by using a Cunningham in the lower luff (fig 4-24).

In all maximum size headsails a Cunningham allows the sail to be cut with the longest possible luff for light airs when area is most needed.

For cross-cut headsails—even those without

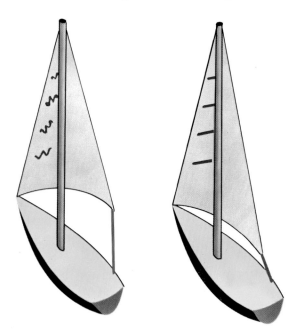

fig 4-23

fig 4-24

and vice versa. On the other hand, by tensioning down on the Cunningham, the head is not moved, and the clew position remains the same.

This is not so relevant to mitred headsails. As the head is raised the more elastic weft allows the leech to stretch nearly as much as the luff. Not, that is, until the sail has to be carried at or above the top limit of its wind range. If the extra tension needed to keep the position of flow forward is applied via the Cunningham, the leech will open, spilling wind which will reduce heel. To achieve this without the Cunningham would mean moving the fairlead aft.

maximum length luffs—there is a further particular benefit to be gained by using a Cunningham. Increasing luff tension (fig 4-25) via the halyard raises the head of the sail (green broken line). The firm-wefted cloth of the cross-cut will not let the leech stretch and so the clew is also raised from (a) to (b). This in turn will mean that the fairlead position has to be moved aft as the wind increases

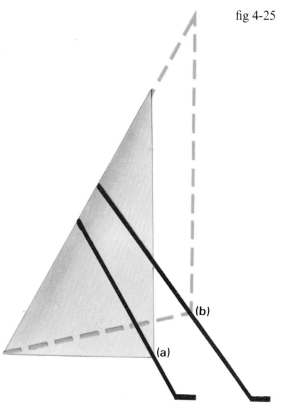

fig 4-25

5 Tuning: the non-masthead rig

Basically there are two types of sailboat rig. Because the sails for each are designed to work according to the characteristics of that particular rig, we must now differentiate between them.

The principle behind the modern masthead form is that the rig should remain rigid, while the sails it supports are adjusted, both in shape and area, to suit the varying conditions. We deal with these in the next chapter.

Prior to the development of modern materials, such as aluminium extrusions and low-stretch wire, this was not practical. The forces generated were too great for the materials at hand. As they had to work within these limitations, it is not difficult to see why designers placed far more emphasis on the mainsail than on the foresail. Mainsail shape could at least be supported on two of its three sides.

This, then, was the accepted rig at the time that sailing dinghies began to appear on the scene.

However, the high performance dinghy brought with it three considerations which have since limited any movement towards the rigid rig, even though the necessary materials are now to hand.

The first is the ratio between the length of the hull, and the height of the mast. If the mast can be supported by means other than stays from the head to bow and stern, a far greater sail area can be carried. Secondly, the vertical force directed downwards by the mast in a rigid-rig, is enormous. For a given sail area, this needs greater stiffness in the hull, which inevitably means more weight. Finally, if the mast is going to remain rigid, the sails must be adjusted around it—and indeed, changed in varying wind forces. On a dinghy, where stability is directly related to crew position, this is impractical, even if the necessary gear could be carried.

Reading this, you might assume that the masthead rig is the ideal, and that the poor dinghy is deprived of the more efficient system. This is by no means true. We have simply used the comparison to highlight the differences between the two rigs.

Whereas new materials have led in one direction to the masthead rig where that is practical, in the case of racing dinghies and keelboats these properties have been harnessed to provide greater efficiency to what is of necessity much the same as the early sail plans.

Indeed, the argument between the relative efficiency of non-masthead and masthead rigs is currently clouded by the increasing number of yachts (fig 5-1) which are reverting to the former.

On the non-masthead rig, the most important sail of the two is the mainsail. This gives more than half of the drive, and it is on the shape of the mainsail that we should first concentrate.

We have seen earlier how the depth of camber in the modern mainsail is controlled by varying the distance between the clew and the luff: increase that distance via the clew outhaul to flatten the sail and vice versa.

However moving the clew is not the only method available for adjusting the distance (red line). By inducing fore and aft bend into the mast (fig 5-2), the mid-luff can be moved forward, thereby increasing the distance from the clew (blue segment).

A combination of both methods of flow control obviously increases the range of wind in which the sail can be made to work effectively.

This is particularly so in the case of dinghies where the forces generated by the wind are relatively low; limited in fact by the weight and power of the crew. The sails can therefore be made of cloth firm enough to resist distortion with the position of flow 'fixed in'. Luff tension as a means of positioning flow assumes a less important role.

fig 5-1

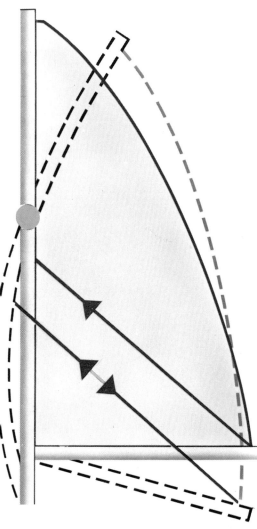

fig 5-2

Mast bend

Herein lies the basic advantage of the non-masthead rig. The mast can be made to bow forward at its mid-point, either by a downward pull via the mainsail leech, as in the simple dinghy rig, or via a permanent backstay on keelboats and yachts.

Let us examine the factors involved in mast bend and for our example use the simplest dinghy rig.

The mast is fixed at its base (fig 5-3). It is also fixed both in the fore and aft plane and sideways plane at the hounds, by the forward pull of the forestay, countered by an aft and lateral pull from the shrouds (red arrows): a simple triangulation of forces. We will return to lateral bend in detail later.

fig 5-3

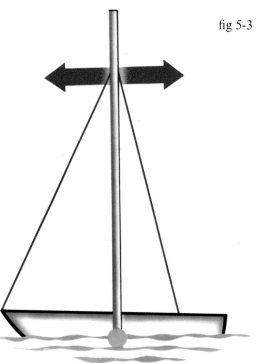

fig 5-6

By increasing tension on the leech with the mainsheet (fig 5-4), a pull in the direction of the red arrow will bend the top part of the spar aft and downwards. At the same time that part of the mast below the hounds will be forced forward into a bow.

Equally, were we to exert forward pressure on the lower section at the gooseneck (fig 5-5) by hardening down on the kicker, or vang, the upper section of the spar would pivot aft.

To induce mast bend, therefore, we have a choice. Either by mainsheet or vang tension; or a combination of both.

The bend characteristics of a particular mast are clearly dependent on its cross section. Nowhere is

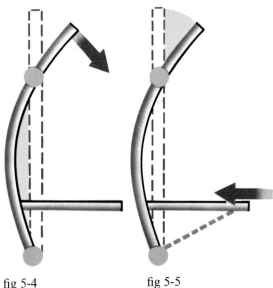

fig 5-4   fig 5-5

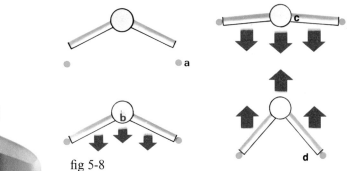

fig 5-8

classes which allow it, a variable mast ram which can be adjusted out on the water. Force in the direction of the arrow increases stiffness.

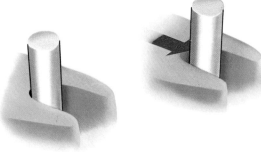

fig 5-7

this more evident than in unstayed spars used on cat-rigs (fig 5-6) where sail flow control is directly related to the bend characteristics of the section.

However the sailor of the more conventional boat has a number of controls with which he can adjust bend and therefore retain the necessary power in his sails. Were the mast to bend excessively—or too easily for the power of the particular crew— then flow in the sail would flatten past its optimum point. At all times the degree of mast bend must be controllable.

The bend in keel stepped masts, which pass through a rectangular hole at deck level—the partners—can be limited by restricting the fore and aft play at that point (fig 5-7). This is done with wedges, prior to going sailing, or for those

Spreaders

An even greater degree of control can be exerted if spreaders are fitted. Aft-raked rigidly mounted spreaders on dinghies and small keelboats limit the degree to which the whole mast can bend by exerting a backward pull on the spar at a point between the heel and the hounds (fig 5-8). They do this by deflecting the shrouds (blue) forward of the straight line (a) they would like to take between their fixed points at the deck and the hounds. This deflection not only restrains the mast from moving forward where the spreaders meet (b), but also stops the backward movement of the upper part of the spar. Swing the spreaders forward (c), and the shroud deflection is increased, further restricting mast bend. If the spreaders are swung aft, towards the natural line of the shrouds (d), the mast will be allowed to develop more bend. Indeed, if they were moved aft past the natural shroud line mast bend would be encouraged when jib tension brought the shrouds under load.

It must be emphasized here however that this type of spreader is only applicable to dinghy and the smallest keelboat rigs. It has proved impractical to control lower mast bend with these on larger keelboats and cruisers. For these boats a lower shroud leading aft from the spreader root to deck level is necessary to provide positive control over fore and aft mast bend. The role of the spreader becomes much more relevant to restricting lateral mast bend by acting as a compression strut between the hounds and the chainplate. This is similar to that played by the spreader in the masthead rig and we deal with it in detail in the next chapter.

Forestay

Reverting to our dinghy example let us examine now the relationship between the shrouds and the forestay.

The method by which forestay tension is induced is one of those fashions which ebbs and flows from class to class at different times in various parts of the world.

The choice is between the 'floppy' system where the jib luff is tightened by hauling the mast and mainsail aft with mainsheet tension, and the rigid system i.e. locking the jib luff tension in against the aft pull of the shrouds.

The latter system has—for the present—emerged as the most universally acceptable and efficient. For this fixed-rake system, the jib halyard must be set up sufficiently tight to lock the mast at the entry sheave point against the aft pull of the shrouds.

Shroud length must be adjusted so that the mast is at its optimum rake for upwind sailing when the jib luff is tensioned. In this way the jib will have a constant degree of luff tension irrespective of the point of sailing. The amount by which the mast is raked in this 'locked in' position has therefore to be a compromise between the perpendicular for off wind sailing, and that degree of aft rake which gives the necessary weather-helm 'feel' for going to windward. With only three or four degrees of heel on the boat for optimum upwind performance, the tiller should have a definite positive 'feel'.

Controls

To sum up therefore we have the following factors governing fore and aft bend, all of which have to be tuned (fig 5-9). The jib forestay or luff wire (a) which holds the mast at the hounds in a fixed position against the aft pull of the shrouds (b). If fitted, the spreaders (c) control the amount by which the lower part of the spar is allowed to bow forward. A similar role is played by the partners (d). Mast bend can be induced by either a downward pull on the mainsheet via the leech to the masthead (e) or a forward push on the lower part of the spar from the vang (f).

This latter is popular as it relieves the mainsheet of much of its vertical loading. With only a directional function to fulfil, a traveller becomes redundant, and a lighter sheet with fewer purchases can be employed to give easier, quicker and more precise control.

fig 4-9

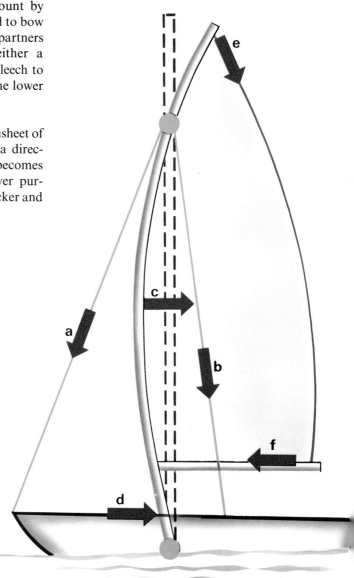

Ashore

To harness mast bend as a control of mainsail shape, it is vital that we now match the spar to the luff curve of the particular sail. The degree to which the flow in the mainsail can be adjusted is relative to the flexibility of the mast within its rig.

To establish the most effective mast bend for your mainsail, turn the rigged boat on to its side (fig 5-10). The mast should be supported at some point along its length to keep the head off the ground. The clew should be pulled out to its black band limit.

Induce mast bending by tightening down on the mainsheet and/or the kicker. As tension is applied, diagonal creases will appear, running from the point of deepest mast curvature down to the clew. Smooth these out by equalizing tension on the luff via the Cunningham (fig 5-11).

Provided that the mast continues to bend, the point will soon be reached when the Cunningham will no longer eliminate the diagonal crease. At that point, that particular mainsail is at its flattest. As it is beneficial to tune the mast as stiff as possible for the designed shape of each sail, there is no point in allowing further mast bend. The

fig 5-10

fig 5-11

spreader tips can be adjusted forward, and/or the forward travel of the mast at deck level limited, so that the mast bending power available on the boat can bring the spar to this point. If on the other hand the spar is set up too rigidly to allow the sail to flatten effectively then further bend can be induced by swinging the spreader tips aft, and if possible increasing the fore and aft travel at the partners.

After these adjustments on shore, it is time to see the effect when sailing. If in 20 knots of wind the combined crew weight is insufficient to keep the boat upright, further mast bend to flatten the sail may be necessary. Retune as above. Conversely, if there is crew weight to spare, mast bend will need to be restricted again—or alternatively a fuller design of sail can be considered.

fig 5-12

Lateral bend

While tuning rig to mainsail, with the boat on its side, it is not necessary to worry about the apparently excessive tension along the leech of the sail. Once sailing, the weight of wind on the sail will open the leech, by bending the unstayed upper section of the mast over to leeward (fig 5-12).

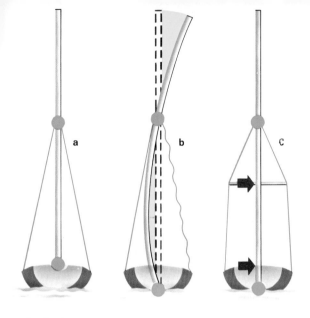

fig 5-13

fig 5-14

This ability of the upper spar to bend sideways also provides the non-masthead rigged boat with an automatic safety valve which spills air once the wind strength has increased past the point where crew weight can keep the boat upright.

Lateral bend is also advantageous on boats with over-lapping headsails. As the topmast falls to leeward, the lower part of the spar bows up to windward widening the slot between the leech of the jib and the mainsail.

However sideways bend in the mast can have a detrimental effect on pointing ability. The aim must be to keep the spar as straight as possible, and certainly until bend can usefully counter heavier winds as outlined. This is the second direction of spar bend which must be tuned (fig 5-13).

Returning to our simple dinghy rig without spreaders, the mast is fixed at two points; the heel and the hounds (a). This is as true for lateral movement as it is for fore and aft. If the mast is keel stepped with partners at deck level, it is important that all sideways movements by the spar is restricted at this point. The inability to bow to windward low down will in turn restrict the degree of leeward bend in the topmast above the hounds, (a and b).

The amount of lateral control which can be exerted of this simply rigged spar is limited. However by introducing spreaders between chainplates and hounds a far greater degree of control can be achieved (c).

The role of the spreader in restricting lateral bend is similar in principle for all boats. For those with non-masthead rigs, the spreader deflects the shroud outwards away from the spar at a point between the hounds and the chainplate. As the windward shroud under load naturally wishes to straighten between the fixed points, so the spreader becomes a compression strut pushing the lower mast down to leeward.

On larger keelboats and non-masthead rigged yachts it is necessary to add lower shrouds (fig 5-14) to support the mast at the spreader root compression point (a). The degree of lateral mast bend is then controlled by the relative tension between the main and lower shrouds in a very similar manner to that outlined for masthead rigs in the next chapter.

On dinghies and smaller keelboats, without lower shrouds, lateral mast bend control is best achieved by adjusting the length of the spreader (fig 5-15). Additional length (yellow) increases the shroud (blue) deflection and restricts bend.

The alternative is to restrict sideways bend by moving the spreaders forward, which increases the distance between the two tips. As this will also restrict fore and aft bend in the mast, a balance has to be struck.

To allow greater lateral bend in the spar under load, reduce the amount by which the shrouds are deflected sideways by the spreaders.

fig 5-15

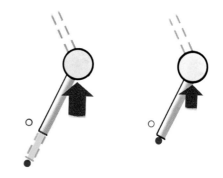

Sail trim

Earlier, we noted that one of the restrictions facing the dinghy sailor was on his freedom of movement within the boat. This is particularly true on the upwind leg, when the crew and helmsman can only view their sail shape and trim from the windward gunwale.

The only way, therefore, to match jib to mainsail and vice versa, is to do it where both people can view the shapes from all angles. In other words, they should be examined on shore.

The boat can be rigged while still strapped tightly down into its trailer. In anything other than light airs, a few extra bodies adding their weight to the windward gunwale will allow you the necessary freedom to walk around. If fitted, a trapeze wire is a great help (fig 5-16).

The boat should be faced into the wind at approximately the same angle as it would be when beating to windward. The mainsail can then be sheeted in and the depth of camber adjusted for optimum flow. Remember the leech tell-tales explained in Chapter 3.

The purpose of this exercise is to match jib to mainsail to give a constant and powerful slot.

Thankfully, for windward work, there is little scope, or indeed need, to keep adjusting the luff of a dinghy jib. The luff wire should be kept as straight as the wind force will allow. Most dinghy jibs are permanently attached to the wire at the head and tack, which effectively locks the position of camber within the sail. However, some are secured at the head by an adjustable lanyard, providing a small amount of flow control.

Easing the lanyard reduces the tension of the cloth relative to the wire so that, although the luff remains straight, the camber can move aft giving a flatter entry to the sail. Tightening the lanyard draws the camber forward.

It is important that, when going to windward, the jib luff should be as tight, and therefore as straight

fig 5-16

fig 5-17

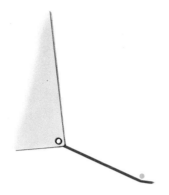

fig 5-18

fig 5-19

as possible in all conditions. It is far better to have a flat jib in light conditions, than to have to cope with fullness in the sail because of excessive luff sag in heavy weather.

Both the depth of camber, and the slot-governing leech of the jib are controlled by sheet tension and the angle at which it is applied to the clew. Whereas on a mainsail you have horizontal and vertical control, on the jib, both functions are performed by a single diagonal pull. While the amount of that pull will govern the distance between the clew and the luff, and therefore the depth of camber in the jib, the direction from which the pull is exerted will control the shape of the leech.

On a boat with fore and aft adjustable fairleads, moving these forward increases the downward component from the sheet. The leech will harden between the head and the clew (fig 5-17). Moving the fairlead aft gives a more horizontal pull allowing the leech to free and twist away to leeward (fig 5-18).

The aim therefore, is to find the fairlead position for each wind strength, which will allow the jib leech to take up a curve which matches that on the leeward side of the mainsail (fig 5-19).

Once this has been achieved for a given wind speed, if the boat has fairleads which can be adjusted laterally, move the sheet and clew towards the centre of the boat until the mainsail is back winded (fig 5-20). The fairlead position should now be noted alongside the relevant wind speed, although it is worth remembering that, once on the water, the apparent wind will be slightly stronger. The

sheet lead may have to be adjusted outboard again to stop excessive back winding.

The rules are therefore: fore and aft adjustment to achieve a slot which is parallel from just below the extreme head of the jib; then lateral adjustment to regulate the slot width. This lateral adjustment can be achieved by moving the fairlead athwartships or by the use of a barber hauler.

Mast-rake

In the special cases where class rules limit jib sheet leads to a precise location, the sheeting angle can only be varied by adjusting the rake of the mast. As the spar rakes aft for upwind sailing, the distance between the head of the jib and the sheet fairlead is reduced. With the 'floppy' system the degree of mast rake is directly related to wind speed. The stronger the wind, the more the rake, the closer the head of the jib comes to the fairlead, the more the jib leech is allowed to free. As the mast returns to the upright in lighter conditions, and off the wind, the leech tightens back up to

fig 5-20

windward. On rigidly locked rigs the same effect can be achieved by raising the jib tack on a strop.

Twist

Because of the relatively short distance between sea level and the head of a dinghy jib, the wind gradient ceases to be an important factor when considering leech twist. It can be ignored completely, in the interests of matching the leech curve to that on the lee of the main. On boats with large, overlapping headsails, the leech can be allowed to twist off to counter excessive lee helm, but this is a relatively rare need and application.

Twist in the upper part of the mainsail is important. In the first chapter we saw that one of the functions of the foresail was to bend the wind into the main, allowing it to be sheeted closer to the boat's centreline.

On the non-masthead rig this effect is limited to the lower section of the mainsail by the height of the jib. Above that point, the main meets the wind on its own, and therefore the sail has to be presented

fig 5-21

fig 5-22

to it at a greater angle. The mainsail for a non-masthead rig is designed with comparatively more fullness at the head and sufficient twist (fig 5-21) must be therefore allowed to develop if flow is to exit cleanly from the leech—and the tell-tales.

As the boat is turned off the wind, the mainsail must be allowed to regain its fuller section. The method will depend on whether bend in the spar has been induced primarily by mainsheet or vang.

If mast bend has been dependent on tension from the vang whilst on the wind, this must be eased. The spar will then straighten, allowing more flow to develop in the sail. At the same time, the Cunningham must be eased to relax the tension along the luff of the sail.

If possible, the clew outhaul should also be eased to induce further fullness into the sail. A series of small, vertical creases (fig 5-22) along the shelf of the foot, serves as a good guide to the limit to

which the clew outhaul should be eased for a particular wind strength.

The primary function of vang tension is now to hold the boom down and thereby stop the leech from falling away. The vang can be pre-tensioned to fulfill this leech control function, prior to the mainsheet being eased. As the boat turns away

fig 5-23

from the wind, it will then only be necessary to balance luff tension with that along the leech by slight adjustment of the Cunningham.

Sail care

Before leaving non-masthead rigs, as we have been primarily concerned with sails made from cloth with a firm, hard finish, a word or two about looking after them. If these sails are to retain their finish, they must be folded after use. On habitable craft, sails present some storage problems, but there is no reason whatever why dinghy sails need to be haphazardly stuffed into their bags.

fig 5-24

A mainsail should be folded or flaked starting at the foot and drawing the rest of the sail towards it in wide folds (fig 5-23).

The luff is folded down on top of itself whilst the leech is allowed to move into the centre. Starting at the clew, the rectangle of flaked sail can then be folded along the foot into a neat roll for bagging.

Mainsails made from very stiff hard cloth benefit from being rolled instead of flaked (fig 5-24). By rolling the sail from head to foot there will be no creases folded into the sail at all. The rolled sail can then be stored in a special tube-like bag.

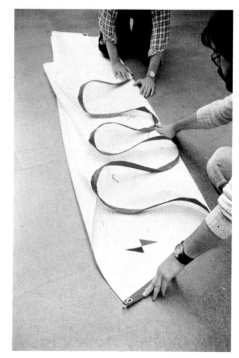

fig 5-25

Jibs can either be rolled, or flaked down (fig 5-25) using long looping folds. Because of the inflexible nature of the 1×19 integral wire used in the luffs, the luff should be allowed to move into the centre of the sail in a series of broad S-bends, whilst the leech is folded down upon itself.

6 Tuning: the masthead rig

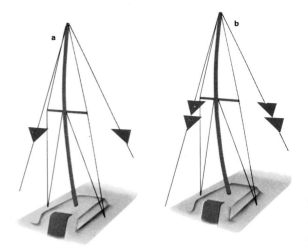

fig 6-1

Few, if any, dinghies have other than non-masthead rigs. Ocean racers, cruisers and keel-boats, on the other hand, have a choice. In this chapter we concentrate on the masthead rig as it applies to bigger boats. However, many of the sail handling and trimming techniques are equally relevant to those boats carrying non-masthead rigs.

As the yacht headsail is so important, let us start there, as one should do in practice, marrying the mainsail to this sail as we proceed.

We have seen the effect of forestay sag on the position and depth of flow in the sail. In anything other than light winds, the forestay, however tight, is going to sag to leeward due to the weight of wind in the sail. However, it soon reaches a point at which a considerable increase in load is necessary to make it sag further. The sailmaker can calculate

and allow for this initial movement when cutting the luff of the sail. However, from that point on, correct flow in the foresail will depend on the tension to which the forestay can be subjected.

On most yachts the conventional method of tensioning the forestay is by moving the masthead aft, via the backstay. However, it is impossible to exert sufficient tension to limit sag to a constant and acceptable degree in all wind strengths, if the mast is allowed to develop any degree of sideways bend, (fig 6-1 (a)).

Further compression will simply increase the bend (fig 6-1 (b)). It is essential, therefore, that the mast be free from lateral bend at all times. This is basically what is meant by tuning the rig.

Whilst still moored, trim the boat to its designed waterline. If the mast is keel-stepped, remove the chocks at deck level and slack off all the shrouds. Now centre the mast athwartships by adjusting the cap-shrouds only. At this stage, do not harden them down. Measuring the distance between the masthead and equal points either side of the boat, with a steel tape-measure hoisted on the main halyard is a good way.

The forestay and backstay can now be adjusted to position the mast in the correct fore and aft plane. The amount of rake depends on personal preference, the balance on the helm while sailing and whether or not the boat is equipped with a backstay which can be easily adjusted while sailing. This is usually accomplished either by (fig

fig 6-2(a, b, c)

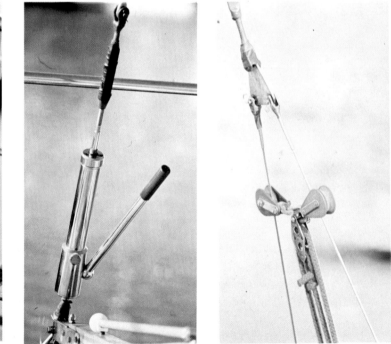

fig 6-3

6-2 (a)) a wheel device, (b) a hydraulic ram or (c) a system of pulleys.

The stays should be adjusted so that when they are at working tension, mast rake is between 2° and 4°. These degrees of mast rake become limits of travel if the backstay is easily adjustable; the spar being more upright for off the wind sailing and raked aft under tension for windward work. If the same working tension is to be used on all points of sailing then the degree of mast rake must be fixed somewhere within these limits. A keel-stepped mast when under working tension should be in firm contact with *aft edge* of the partner hole at deck level (fig 6-3 (a)). If not, the mast heel position will have to be adjusted until it is.

The cap shrouds can now be fully tensioned with equal turns on both turnbuckles (rigging screws) until they are really taut. Check athwartship position of masthead again with the steel tape-measure. The masthead is now in position. At this stage, the spar is chocked very firmly into the *centre* of its hole at deck level, (fig 6-3 (b)). This achieves a slight bowing effect in the spar which in fact makes it more rigid. Hand tighten any slackness out of the lower shrouds, and, if fitted, intermediate shrouds, and we are ready to go sailing.

Put the boat hard on the wind under full sail in sufficient wind to make it heel between 20° and 25°.

By looking up along the mainsail groove you can easily ascertain any lateral bend which might be developing. If the centre of the mast is sagging to leeward, (fig 6-4 (a)) tighten down on the windward lower shroud(s) until the spar straightens. If it is bowing up to windward, (fig 6-4 (b)) slacken off on the windward shroud(s). Masts with more than single spreaders could, of course, exhibit a combination of bends in either direction, each of which must be adjusted out with the relevant lower or intermediate windward shroud. In this case, always work from the top downwards, getting the intermediates right before tackling the lowers.

However many spreaders are fitted, one principle remains; do not adjust either cap shroud.

fig 6-4

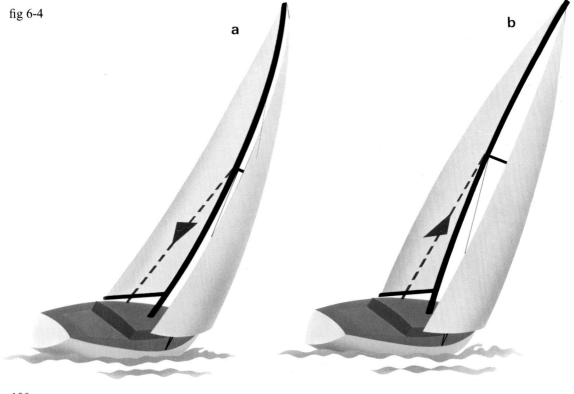

a

b

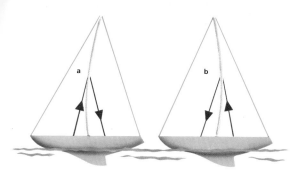

fig 6-5

On boats rigged with twin lower shrouds, you must now look up the side of the mast. If it is bowing forward at spreader height (fig 6-5 (a)), slack off on the forward and take down on the aft lower until the spar is straight. Reverse the procedure if the mast bows aft (fig 6-5 (b)). Check to see if these adjustments have affected lateral bend, and if so, straighten the spar out again by equal amounts of adjustment on both windward lowers. On boats with single lowers and a baby stay, the job is somewhat simpler. Leave the baby stay off until all lateral bend has been eliminated. Then it can be used to prevent the mast flexing and for small fore and aft adjustments.

Once you are satisfied, tack the boat and carry out exactly the same operation on the other side of the rig.

Unfortunately, it is only after all this effort that you will be able to see if the cap-shrouds were tensioned sufficiently before you left your mooring. If, with the windward rigging nicely holding the mast straight, the leeward shrouds are excessively floppy, you are almost back to square

one. Tighten down on the cap shrouds by the same number of turns on each side, and then start all over again to balance the lowers and inter-mediates.

Once you are happy with the rig, the turnbuckles, and for that matter all other sharp surfaces must be bound with PVC sticky tape. Sailmakers know only too well the damage caused to expensive sails by unnoticed corners and pins on deck.

One final point to remember: wire, and even rod, does stretch. The rig is nicely set up now. But it will need re-doing two or three times during an average season, so check regularly.

Grooved headstays

Our aim, so far, has been a tight forestay. Perhaps now is the moment to take a look at an interesting development: the grooved headstay.

Originally these were stainless steel rods in-corporating a single groove into which ran a small diameter plastic luff 'rope'. The aim being a more aerodynamic luff than the traditional hanks. This may have been true, but it was not long before racing sailors saw a much more important oppor-tunity. If two grooves could be incorporated, when the time came to change sails, the new one could be hoisted, and sheeted in before the old one was taken down.

Prior to that, and still the case with boats equipped with hanks, the quickest way to change was to hank the new sail to the bottom of the forestay and then lower the old sail, snatching hanks and halyard off as they came down. Only then could the new sail be hoisted and sheeted home, and however well drilled the crew, for a time the boat was inevitably bareheaded.

With the advent of the twin grooved forestay, the decision to change sails became an easy one. Of course it does mean that twin halyards and tack fittings have become necessary.

There is one major drawback to the system. When a foresail fitted with hanks is dropped, it remains attached to the forestay: very important for the cruising man. A groove-luff headsail on the other hand has to be collected as it comes down, and secured (fig 6-6) on deck or taken below.

Grooved headstays come in a variety of sizes and shapes but there are two basic types. The twin grooves can be side by side (fig 6-7), or on opposite edges (fig 6-8) of the foil. In the latter case, the foil has to swivel, and indeed most of the side-by-side foils do this as well. The support is provided by the

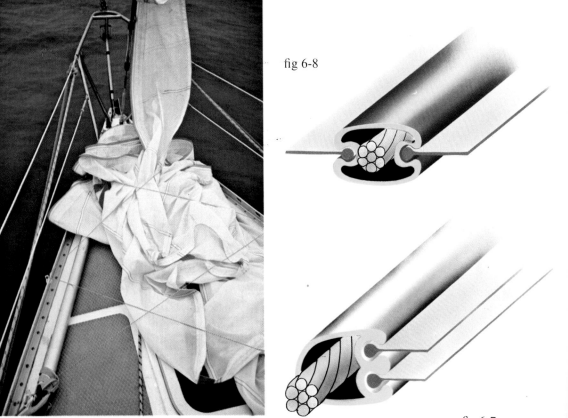

fig 6-8

fig 6-7

fig 6-6

wire or rod forestay which runs up inside the foil section.

Of the two, the side-by-side system is the best (fig 6-9). With the rotating foil going through 180° each time a sail is changed, a certain clarity of thought is necessary from the crew as to exactly how many twists each halyard has made on its twin as they emerge from their masthead sheaves. Whichever system is used, with twin halyards it has become a routine for foredeck crew to check for halyard twist everytime a sail is lowered.

fig 6-9

The advantage of the twin groove foil for the cruising man is that two headsails can be flown down wind: much easier to handle than a spinnaker. Indeed for racing boats in very heavy weather this is equally relevant; two headsails, each flown on opposite sides of the foil give an enviable degree of control and stability compared with a spinnaker. In both cases there would appear to be an advantage in the opposite groove type of foil, although twin sails can work in a side-by-side system.

Stowage

No sailmaker likes to think of his sails being stuffed any old how into their bags after use, but if he is realistic, he knows that this is exactly what happens most of the time. One benefit brought about by headfoils is that headsails have to be prepared for hoisting again before they are packed into their bags. The racing community have

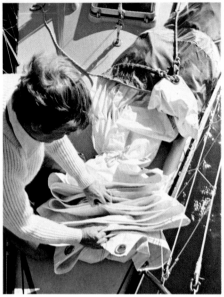

fig 6-10

developed the quickest and easiest method possible. The crewman packing the sail runs one hand from tack to head folding the luff tape into a concertina in his other hand (fig 6-10). He then secures this concertina with a sail tie and works the sail from luff to clew into three folds. If a 'sausage' type bag is being used it is dropped on to the base of the bag and the zip secured over. If the sail is going into a conventional bag, another concertina is made.

When the time comes to hoist the sail the clew, tack and head are immediately to hand and there can be no chance of the luff being twisted.

Sheets can be attached to the sail whilst it is still in its bag, or it can be stretched out along the deck, as long as the tape securing the luff is left on until the last minute. It is also very important when hoisting

fig 6-11

a sail into a headfoil that the whole of the flaked luff should be as far forward under the foil feeder as is possible (fig 6-11).

Whether a foil or conventional hanks are used, the next requirement for a modern tape-luff headsail is sufficient power to tension that luff correctly.

Luff tension

This is an area of very common misunderstanding. Most yachtsmen simply do not believe that their sails are designed to withstand enormous loads on the luff. Unless those loads are applied, the sail will not take on its power producing shape.

The table (fig 6-12) shows the sort of halyard loads on a range of yachts as estimated by a leading winch manufacturer. The right hand column shows the power ratio, i.e. the number of times available man-power is multiplied by the time it

reaches the drum, of recommended halyard winches. The power ratio figure is used by this manufacturer to number their range in an easily understandable way. Whilst these loads were estimated for masthead rigs, there would be little difference in those experienced by non-masthead yachts. And remember, to transmit these sorts of loads from deck level to masthead, wire halyards are essential.

Having acquired the power to adjust the tension of the luff under load, we must now establish the points of maximum and minimum stretch for each sail and calibrate the halyard at deck level accordingly.

Full size racing sails should have the maximum possible luff length so that when stretched for the upper limit of their wind range, they neatly fit the available luff length of the particular boat, i.e. between halyard shackle and tack fitting. By

fig 6-12

BOAT SIZE (LOA metres)	HALYARD LOADS	WINCH (power ratio/size)
25 to 29 ft **7.6 to 8.25** (¼ TON)	**350 Kg** 800 lb	16
30 to 32 ft **9.1 to 9.75** (½ TON)	**600 Kg** 1400 lb	30
33 to 35 ft **10 to 10.7** (¾ TON)	**700 Kg** 1600 lb	40
35 to 39 ft **10.7 to 12** (1 TON)	**1000 Kg** 2200 lb	42

hoisting the shackle to the masthead sheave, you should have a very good reference point for maximum hoist. Under load, the halyard will stretch ensuring that the swage does not enter the masthead sheave.

Incidently, we strongly recommend that halyards be made of flexible galvanized wire, rather than the smarter stainless steel wire which 'work hardens' and eventually becomes extremely brittle.

At maximum hoist, the wire halyard should be permanently marked to line up with a reference point on either the mast or deck. Sails with less than full length luffs (fig 6-13) can each have a wire strop (blue) added at the head so that the same maximum hoist position applies for all sails.

When marking the halyard: sticky tape or seizings are of little use; they quickly move or wear as they pass through blocks or sheaves.

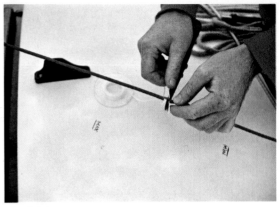

fig 6-14

The best way is to open the lay of the wire with a fid (fig 6-14) and pass a whipping twine seizing actually through the wire.

With the maximum sail hoisted and slackened off until horizontal wrinkles appear in the luff, it is now possible to mark either mast or deck with a minimum hoist reference point. These minimum and maximum points are important. They give the sail trimmer a reference within which to work. Much has been written on tabulating the distances in between these two, so that exact tensions can be duplicated on future occasions. We are doubtful of the value of this practice. As long as the sailor has the confidence of knowing his maximum and minimum tensions and can relate this scope to what he sees by looking at his sails, we believe he is going to produce an effective sail shape to cope with the particular condition facing him. It is far better than referring blindly to past notes.

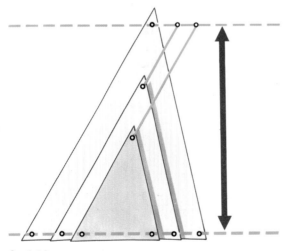

fig 6-13

Of course this does not mean that one should not note the effects on boat speed from different tensions in differing conditions. Once the sail is set up with the draft in the theoretically correct position, if the boat picks up speed or points higher in flat water when halyard tension is eased; note the fact and remember it next time you are faced with those conditions. Each boat has its own pattern of behaviour, and it is the ability to discover and remember that pattern, that singles out the good sailor.

As we have already seen, the position of maximum flow in the headsail—ideally between one third and half way back from the luff, is kept there by alternately adjusting the tension of the halyard and sheet. In the case of the cross-cut headsail, the position of the sheet lead may also need adjustment. Once the position and depth of flow have been established, the tip of the leeward spreader is the best reference point when trimming sheet and halyard tension (fig 6-15).

For instance, if the breeze drops slightly, unless halyard and sheet are eased, flow will move forward in the sail, flattening the aft trailing edge (fig 6–16). Were the wind to increase with still no adjustment, flow would move aft, widening the gap between sail and spreader (fig 6-17). This would be particularly true in the case of a mitred sail with its more elastic leech.

fig 6-15   fig 6-16   fig 6-17

The mainsail

Turning our attention to the mainsail, we have two effects in mind. The mainsail must be married into the flow pattern already set up by the headsail. Secondly, it must be trimmed to balance the helm of the boat going to windward. The best position from which to view the slot between headsail and mainsail is from as far aft as possible on the leeward quarter.

It is difficult to set down a precise sequence of action aimed at producing the perfect slot. Whichever sail one starts with will almost certainly have to be re-adjusted once the second has been trimmed to match, and so on.

Take the mainsail as a starting point. In a fair breeze; medium to full camber is trimmed into the sail via the clew outhaul. In this moderate wind, the wind gradient is negligible so twist is not necessary and the mainsheet can be hardened down (fig 6-18).

As the wind lightens, the wind gradient does become a factor; so the necessary twist to take advantage of this can be eased in with the mainsheet (fig 6-19). The clew outhaul is also eased to give a little more camber.

Having set the main, the position and degree of camber in the headsail can then be adjusted for the wind strength. Once this is achieved, if the slot does not appear parallel, then a slight compromise has to be sought. Either the shape of the headsail leech can be altered by juggling sheet tension with fairlead position; or the camber in the main can be

fig 6-18

fig 6-19

fig 6-20   fig 6-21   fig 6-22

re-adjusted using a combination of clew outhaul and mainsheet. Some idea of the variety of slot balancing adjustments and their effects can be seen from these pictures (fig 6-20, 21, 22).

The best indication of the optimum slot width is from the luff of the main. In light winds, the leech of the headsail can be pulled closer to the centre line to close the slot. In heavier weather, the mainsheet traveller should be eased to leeward once the slot shape has been established. In either case, the optimum point is just before the main luff lifts to windward. This is not the effect of luffing in the true sense. You have simply reached the point where the flow on the windward side of the headsail has refused to compress and accelerate

any more and has backwinded the main. From this point on, the main will progressively backwind and one has to make a fine judgement. If there is still excessive weather helm, then the sail must be flattened along the foot and then let further down to leeward. If this does not relieve pressure on the helm without backwinding the main, then it is time to reef.

The mainsail is unique. It is the only sail on a yacht which must cope with all wind strengths and directions. When one considers this, it becomes clear that how the sail is to be reefed becomes one of its most important design criteria. Important enough in fact to have formed the basis of the giant steps forward since the early 70s.

One thing was certain. Roller reefing, where the sail was rolled down around a revolving boom, was not the answer. It reduced the sail area all right, but it was virtually impossible to maintain the foot tension as the sail was rolled in.

The need to maintain clew tension even with a reef is fundamental to the modern mainsail, and has led to the almost universal readoption of slab reefing. Readoption because it is a very similar, although much tidied up, system to that used by our grandfathers.

These days, the sail is equipped with luff and leech cringles at each reefing level up the sail (fig 6-23). Simple hooks will be provided either side of the gooseneck to take alternate luff cringles; and two pennants (red and blue lines) are led from the inner end of the boom, where they can always be reached, out to adjustable leads on either side of the boom end.

fig 6-24

fig 6-23

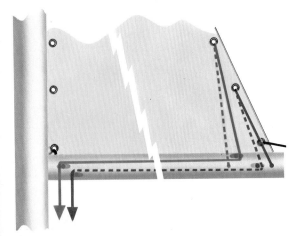

Only two pennants are necessary however many reefs are fitted as they can alternatively be re-rove through the next reef cringle. The end of the pennant is then reattached to the boom. There are a number of variations on this theme, some lines are led through the boom internally, whilst on other boats it is preferred to lead each pennant along the side of the boom where it is visible for signs of wear.

Whichever way is used, it is important to find the correct position for the leads or stops before the reefs are used in earnest. When the cringle is actually down on the boom the pull from the pennant should bisect the angle between boom and leech when the mainsheet is hardened in. This can only be done by trial and error. There is a real danger that too much pull in one direction could stretch and permanently damage the sail. On this boat (fig 6-24) the reef pennants emerge through jambers at the gooseneck and lead to winches close to that for the main halyard. Two men at the mast can reach everything.

fig 6-25

fig 6-26

In operation, the system is simplicity itself. To tie in a reef, one man eases the main halyard. If the winch is close to the gooseneck, he can also hook on the luff cringle as soon as it is lowered far enough. Once the luff is hooked on (fig 6-25), he tensions the halyard preferably to a premarked position. During this short period the boom is held by either a topping-lift if fitted, a mechanical or hydraulic boom vang, or by the helmsman or trimmer taking up excessive slack on the mainsheet. Whilst the halyard is being re-tensioned, the second reefing crewman pulls on the leech reefing line using a winch for the final foot or so if necessary (fig 6-26).

fig 6-27

Headsail reefing

The cross-cut headsail, as we have seen, employs exactly the same design principles as the mainsail.

Consequently, the sailor, when faced with the need to shorten sail forward, now has an alternative to changing to a smaller jib. He can simply reef the one already hoisted.

The only equipment needed apart from the mainsail-type reefing cringles at luff and leech, is a spare sheet; an extra sheet fairlead, twin tack hooks (fig 6-29) and possibly a sheet stopper, but this latter is not vital.

This simple system is really the only way that the sail area can be reduced satisfactorily (fig 6-27) and just as important, the camber in the sail flattened. Compare the thin section of sail (see it there?), on the left of the mast (fig 6-28) with that in illustrations (3-21, 22, 23).

fig 6-28

One point however that is worth remembering. There is nothing sacred about getting the clew cringle right down to the boom. Once it is past the point of solely downward pull i.e. the foot is being stretched as well, then the pennant provides an infinitely variable adjustment for mainsail camber.

When shaking out a reef, the procedure works in reverse: ease the pennant—this has to be done first, otherwise even when the halyard is slackened, the foot tension will make it impossible to unhook the luff cringle. Ease the halyard; unhook the luff cringle; take up on the halyard.

fig 6-29

fig 6-30

The new sheet is led from aft through the spare fairlead already positioned correctly for the reefed sail. Even on very large boats the height of the reef cringle should not be out of reach. If it is very high, an open-hooked length of stainless steel rod may be necessary to reach the cringle. The working sheet is started to relieve pressure on the headstay and the halyard eased until the luff cringle can be attached to the spare tack hook. After the halyard is re-tensioned, the new sheet is winched home (fig 6-30). When shaking out this reef, be very careful to ease the sheet well before hauling up on the halyard—particularly if a headfoil system is being used. Any pull aft on the sail will surely jam the feeder.

Changing headsails

The traditional way to shorten headsail area is, of course, to change to a smaller, flatter sail. This process has been revolutionized, as we have already mentioned, by the introduction of twin grooved headfoils which allow the replacement sail to be hoisted and sheeted in, before the old sail is lowered. The system appears to be self explanatory, but there are pitfalls to trap the unwary. Experience on racing boats has in many instances uncovered more efficient ways of doing things.

Obviously a twin groove headfoil system means a doubling up of all associated equipment. Double headsail halyards, tack fixings, sheet fairleads, halyard and sheet winches, or at least a system whereby an old line can be stopped off leaving a winch free for its twin.

It is certainly worth colour coding the twin systems with a simple red for port and green for starboard code. If the port halyard clip, tack hook and foil feeder groove are all marked with the same colour and this corresponds to a similarly marked rope halyard-tail further aft, a great many of the pitfalls and tangles associated with twin headfoils will be avoided.

Opinions differ as the best side on which to hoist the new sail. Assuming one has the choice of tacks, is it better to feed the new sail in when the spare groove is to windward than to leeward? On the face of it, the answer seems simple enough: It must be easier to hoist in the windward groove (fig 6-31). Easy that is until one tries to take the old sail down, under and to leeward of the new one (fig 6-32). Certainly it is much more difficult to feed a new sail under the old one, up into a leeward spare

fig 6-31

fig 6-32

groove. On the other hand, once it is up, the old sail comes down very easily cradled by the new one to leeward.

There is one answer which makes the best of both worlds and though it may sound daring, is, in practice, beautifully straightforward.

Hoist the new sail whilst the spare groove is to windward. Once it is up and the halyard cleated off, go about. The old sail is now to windward and when released should slide sweetly to the foredeck.

And just a word about sheets while changing. The normal system while changing on the same tack is to reeve a third sheet on to the new sail through a suitably placed lead on the leeward side. This is used to sheet the new sail in; the old sail's weather sheet being transferred to the new sail in due course. When changing sail 'on the tack', the windward sheet is transferred from the old to the new sail before hoisting—someone having also remembered to change the weather fairlead for the new sail—and that's that. Once hoisted and tacked, the new sail—now to leeward—cradles the old sail until it is lowered. The lazy weather sheet can then be transferred to the new sail.

So far we have been concerning ourselves solely with sail handling on the wind. However, these same fore and aft sails have to provide power through the reach to the run for most cruising yachtsmen, and even for the spinnaker-set the wind has to retreat some little way before the kite can be flown.

Once the sheets have been eased on any yachts with an overlapping headsail, a significant change occurs in the relationship between the two sails.

fig 6-33

From here on round, the mainsail is going to assert itself as the increasingly dominant partner. For one thing, as the boat turns in relation to the wind, the mainsail is progressively becoming the sail the wind meets first. Secondly, because it is held in shape at the clew as well as tack and head, the main can be presented to the apparent wind at a constantly efficient shape. This is not the case for the overlapping headsail. All that happens when the jib sheet is eased, is that the body of the sail fills out to leeward and the leech falls away. Ideally one would want a spacer, similar to the main boom, running from headsail tack to clew to stretch the camber out and hold the leech down.

The best one can do in the circumstances if the boat is equipped with inboard sheet lead tracks, is to rig a spare reaching sheet (fig 6-33 and 34) from the clew of the headsail, outside the lifelines, to a snatch-block fairlead outboard and forward of the windward sheeting position. The aim of moving the lead forward is to stop the leech of the sail falling away. This is inevitable at the top of the sail—the sheeting base even right outboard is just too narrow.

Whatever happens, do not be tempted to trim either sail for a nice looking slot. The main is trimmed as full as possible with luff and foot eased, provided it does not cause excessive weather helm. The kicking strap is always tightened to minimize twist. On a close reach, the mainsheet might have to be eased to help weather helm, but that is all. As far as the headsail is concerned, one should always trim the sheet to keep the tell-tales on both sides of the sail streaming aft.

fig 6-34

7 Spinnakers

By now the reader will be too well versed in the principles of flow over the surface of each sail to need much reminding of the theory set out in the first chapter. Sails power the boat not by offering resistance to the wind, but by deflecting its flow.

This principle applies to spinnakers in exactly the same way as it does to fore and aft sails, even though to the unfamiliar they may seem to catch the wind in a bag and thereby pull the boat forward.

The power in the spinnaker is dependent on the proportion of its area over which it is possible to develop a dynamic surface flow.

There is however one vital difference between the spinnaker and the fore and aft sail. That is in the direction of the flow.

As the boat is turned progressively away from the wind the main and jib sheets are eased so that the angle at which each sail meets the wind remains constant; thereby allowing the flow to remain attached across the width of each sail. Once the apparent wind is on the beam, it is time to consider hoisting a spinnaker which will greatly increase the amount of sail area over which flow can be generated. On this point of sailing (fig 7-1) the spinnaker works in exactly the same way as a headsail with flow remaining parallel to the surface of the water, provided there is not excessive heel. However as the boat turns from a reach to a run, the tack and luff of the sail are brought progressively round; and the wide head of the spinnaker is presented to the wind. The flow deflected by the head is directed downwards over the spinnaker, and this downward component in

fig 7-1

119

Once the combination of these two flow directions is firmly grasped it becomes much easier to understand some of the basic aspects of the spinnaker design and trim.

Cloth

Modern spinnaker cloth is a direct result of the extensive developmental effort over the years into the weaving of nylon fabric for parachutes. The

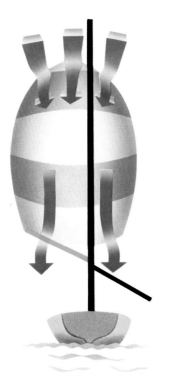

fig 7-2

fig 7-3

the flow progressively increases as the sail is trimmed further and further aft. By the time the boat is on a dead run with the spinnaker tack as far aft as it will go, the downward flow from the head (fig 7-2) has virtually taken over from the lateral flow across the sail.

In smooth conditions this effect can be seen by the rippling effect on the water below the foot produced by the down-flow. The effect also becomes obvious when the sheet and guy are released and spinnaker allowed to fly free (fig 7-3). The down-flow forces the body of the sail towards the horizontal.

120

fig 7-4

properties sought after are very similar: light weight, strength, elasticity to absorb shock loadings, controlled porosity and restricted cross weave distortion. The problems associated with the latter are as relevant to spinnaker shape and its control under load as they are with fore and aft sails, as we will see when we come to discuss the relevant shapes and constructions.

Nylon has a number of interesting qualities which make it ideal for spinnakers. The fine dernier yarns are bulkier for a given weight and strength than for example, polyester, enabling them to fill the gaps in the weave more effectively, thereby restricting the amount of air that can seep through. The fabric can be made virtually impermeable by a coating of polyurethane on the surface which gives the cloth its crisp finish. More important, this coating locks the weave together decreasing its ability to stretch diagonally across the bias, and increasing its ability to spring back once load comes off the sail.

The shock loading experienced when a spinnaker fills in a strong wind is enormous (fig 7-4). A sail of

the same size made, again for example from polyester with little give, would demand handling gear of truly massive proportions.

While polyurethane coating is popular there are others. For example melamine and other resins are used to impregnate some spinnaker nylon although their recovery characteristics are not as good. At the other extreme some remarkably hard finishes (fig 7-5) have been developed which maintain a very high degree of dimensional stability, up to a critical loading. This hard finish is popular for high performance dinghy spinnakers where a particular shape, once built into the sail, will remain constant under the relatively low-load. However once the finish breaks down—and under severe usage it breaks down very quickly—the sail becomes useless. A top competitive sailor can expect to get through several such sails during a racing season.

fig 7-5

Tearing is another problem directly related to the hardness of the finish. The lattice-like network of darker squares across the surface of the fabric are extra—and sometimes stronger—yarns woven in at regular intervals along the warp and the weft to prevent rips developing (fig 7-6). Commonly known as Ripstop, in practice these have little effect once a tear has started. However if the cloth has a soft finish, the yarns when subjected to a point of pressure, bunch together sharing the load. A tear is much more difficult to start, than if each yarn is held apart by a hard finish and can be broken individually.

As we shall see shortly, the search for more and more efficient spinnaker shape has led to more and more complex design and manufacturing techniques. Transforming the nylon from rolls of cloth into fair three-dimensional curves has taken the designer into the complex realms of spherical

fig 7-7

fig 7-6

122

geometry far more complicated than those demanded by fore and aft sails.

This has in turn led to the use of the computer by those sailmakers in the vanguard of spinnaker fabrication.

So much so, that today, the best sails never see the traditional loft floor until, completed, they are laid out for pre-delivery checking. Each panel is individually cut out (fig 7-7), using a hot roller knife which seals the weave. Each is then numbered to a complex sewing code and passed to a machinist who joins them all together (fig 7-8).

fig 7-8

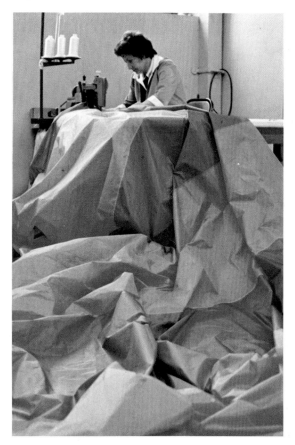

Shape

Turning to spinnaker shapes and remembering the change in the direction of the flow over the sail from across when reaching to vertical when dead running, how do we achieve the optimum shape? The answer has to be a compromise, particularly in the case of a dinghy spinnaker which has to be equally effective on a reach and a run—and indeed all points in between when there is flow both laterally and vertically. In the case of the yacht where spinnakers can be changed as easily as headsails the compromise is not so important—they can carry both running and reaching spinnakers as well as a selection of weights and shapes suitable for different wind strengths. The trend even on yachts is towards compromise shapes designed for all conditions, partly to reduce costs and partly for the increased convenience.

The compromise is further dictated by the racing class rules which control symmetry and the relationship between height and girth of each spinnaker (fig 7-9 and 10). However for the purposes of seeking the ideal shape—if such a thing exists—let us ignore that factor and imagine no such outside influence on pure sail shape.

The modern spinnaker is controlled so that both sides are symmetrical. This in turn means that the shape of each vertical half has to be just as efficient as a flow exit as it is as a flow entry. In fact more so, as one of the fundamental laws of spinnaker design and trim is that it is more important to let the airflow out effectively than it is to get it in.

fig 7-10

fig 7-9

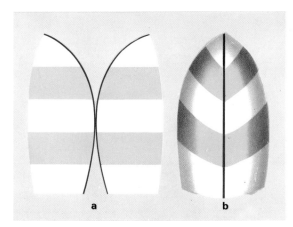

a   b

fig 7-11

Until the early Sixties spinnakers were made from two identical halves, the panels on each side being simply sewn together along parallel edges with no attempt at individual shaping (fig 7-11 (a)). The two sides were then joined down a shaped central seam (b). The result was a cross-section with a deeper camber in the centre, particularly across the upper part of the sail. The curve over which flow had to be coaxed was neither fair horizontally, nor vertically. To use every inch of available surface the spinnaker should correspond in shape to that on the outside of a sphere (fig 7-12). Peeling an orange gives a good idea of the principle.

Ideally whilst still on a reach one wants the spinnaker to be relatively flat, particularly high in the sail to minimize the heeling force. In effect the sail is simply acting as a larger area headsail.

On a run the sail has to be vertically as full as possible to take advantage of the downward flow. In plan form this ideal spinnaker will be wide at the top to catch the maximum amount of air. However, on a reach those same wide shoulders will cause excessive heel.

Not too many years ago the only answer was an unsatisfactory compromise between the two. Today, by developing cuts which exploit the natural characteristics of woven nylon the sailmaker is able to provide the sailor with a spinnaker which when trimmed correctly will do both jobs equally well.

Let us take for our example a simple spinnaker for a dinghy where the shape compromises are most evident, but where the lesser forces involved make an answer more practical.

fig 7-12

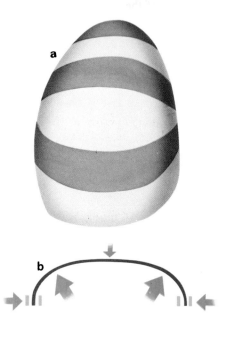

fig 7-14

fig 7-13

Spherical spinnakers were made by running panels across the width of the sail, tapering each edge to produce the required curve (fig 7-13 (a)). The pull on tack and clew across the bias of the panels allows uniform fullness to develop in the body of the sail under load. Pull at the head is restrained by the line of the weft passing down the centre line of the sail (fig 7-13 (b)), thereby preventing fullness where it is not wanted. Very important if the flow is to be kept moving over this wide area of cloth.

On the other hand the pull away from the head close to the leeches (medium arrows) meets little resistance to stretch as it is across the bias of the fabric. At the extreme edge stretch (green) is restricted by the leech tapes with the result that fullness develops in the shoulders creating a powerful elliptical shape.

For small spinnakers, this cross-cut design, together with the later radial-head development, offers excellent all-round performance.

However the experience gained by leading sail-makers in the development of the tri-radial spinnakers, when applied to dinghy and other dayboat classes is beginning to show similar performance advantages to those already proven on larger yachts (fig 7-14).

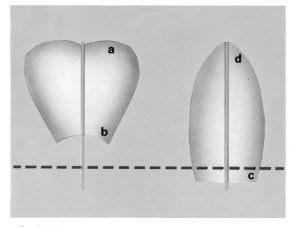

fig 7-15

Shape control

With the wind well aft of the beam the downward flow component will make the spinnaker want to rise (fig 7-15). At the same time the flow in the middle of the sail will draw the two edges closer together increasing the depth of camber across the sail. By easing the sheet and raising the tack the shoulders of the sail will now widen—spreading the sail's wings (a); whilst the tack and clew will come closer to each other to achieve a funnelling effect for the downward flow (b). Turning on to a broad reach the horizontal pull between clew and tack becomes stronger, flattening the camber in the lower part of the sail (c). Because the upper section of this size of spinnaker has so much fullness built into it, downward tension at tack and clew will tighten luff and leech increasing the camber at the head and therefore the heeling moment. When the wind strength increases the answer therefore is to raise the foot of the sail as high as possible so that the edges of the sail at the top flatten out the camber and allow the wind to

fig 7-17

fig 7-16

escape. This is only possible with dinghy sails where the boat can be kept upright on a spinnaker reach by a combination of crew weight and dynamic stability of a planing hull (fig 7-16). Once a displacement boat has started to roll the transverse flow actually moves upwards into the spinnaker increasing pressure on the upper part of the sail, and accelerating the roll (fig 7-17).

That is not the only reason why yacht spinnaker design and trim demands a somewhat different approach.

First of all, the forces all round are very much greater, yet the inherent stability of the available fabric is limited. Secondly development has been largely dictated by the International Offshore Rule with its relatively greater height to width ratio. Masthead rig spinnakers tend to be tall and narrow.

Whereas the sailmaker can achieve a high degree of control by building shape into a dinghy spinnaker, this is much harder to do for an ocean racing sail. He has therefore to build in one shape which will stretch under load into the desired effect.

The classic running spinnaker for a displacement boat can be similar in construction to that of the simple dinghy sail. However, due to the complex loadings on the acutely tapered panels near the head, it became popular to replace these with a series of narrow tapered panels which radiate down into the body of the sail. Each radial panel has its warp yarn running along its length, thereby giving total shape stability to the upper part of the sail by equalizing stretch in all directions from the head.

At the other two points of attachment, the clew and the tack, pressure in the middle of the sail as the wind increases, causes 'collapse' similar to that in a genoa, but to a very much greater degree. The body of the sail fills out drawing the leech and luff towards the foot and vice versa. See what is happening to this beautifully setting spinnaker (fig 7-18). The convex curve along the foot has disappeared up into the body of the sail and the leech has taken on a concave section. The body of the sail has blossomed.

This type of sail is not suitable for reaching in anything more than the lightest breeze. The fullness which automatically develops in the body of the spinnaker from the lower corners—and from the upper one before radial heads were developed—is excessive and will overpower the boat. The wide shoulders built in to the sail for

fig 7-18

running further restrict its use for reaching as it is impossible to flatten the upper part of the sail.

Starcut

It was the search for the answer to this problem at the Banks Sarisbury loft in the early Sixties which led to the development of the Starcut reaching sail (fig 7-19).

By extending the radial cut principle from all three corners so that warp yarn radiated along the panels fanwise into the body of the sail in the same direction as the stresses, they were able for the first time to eliminate distortion under load throughout the centre body of the sail. The vertical flow could be flattened by increasing the vertical component in sheet and guy tension, whilst the

fig 7-19

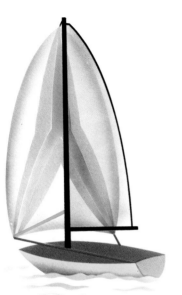

fig 7-20

Tri-radial

Since the 'invention' of the Starcut a compromise running/reaching design has developed which is now extremely popular; due largely to the convenience factor. It attempts, quite successfully, to make the best of both worlds by using radial panels at all three corners, but leaving cross-cut panels in the middle height of the spinnaker (fig 7-21). It remains to be seen what develops from this Tri-radial cut.

fig 7-21

horizontal flow up and down the height of the sail could be controlled with the horizontal components.

Such was the breakthrough of this construction for reaching spinnakers that during the season after they were introduced in 1968, as soon as the British Admiral's Cup team was chosen, their captain insisted that each skipper acquire a Starcut before the competition.

The trimming technique for the Starcut is somewhat different to that used whilst reaching with a running spinnaker. As loading will not vary the camber due to the more stable construction the pole height becomes critical. Too high and it will flatten the sail. The pole is invariably set lower for the Starcut and the sheet lead then brought forward to level out the clew (fig 7-20).

fig 7-22

Trim

The basic techniques for optimum spinnaker trim will now be spelt out. The tack of the sail is attached to the end of the spinnaker pole which moves in a radius around the mast controlled by the guy. The height of the tack is governed by a topping lift, which leads to a point further up the mast and thence down to deck level from where it can be adjusted; and a fore guy, which on a small boat leads from a point on or near the mast at deck level. On dinghies it is usual for this downhaul to be partly strong elastic shockcord so that it does not have to be adjusted every time the pole is moved. It is important that this should incorporate a stop which limits the upward travel of the boom during a broach. The forces on a yacht spinnaker pole are considerably greater. It is normal therefore to lead the foreguy to a point near the bow before bringing it aft. This also provides a three-point anchorage to lock the pole end in position. Even then the strain holding the spinnaker down is considerable and it is worth considering a two-to-one purchase system. Such a double length foreguy leads from along one side of the boat, through a double block near the bow, up through a block on the pole end, back through the second sheave of the deck block and along the

other side of the vessel (fig 7-22). This has an added advantage. The downhaul can also always be adjusted from the weather side of the boat.

The inboard end of the pole is attached to the mast, on a dinghy and small keelboat to a fixed ring; whilst on a larger boat the attachment point can normally be adjusted vertically so that whatever the height of the tack end, the pole can be kept horizontal thereby exposing the maximum spinnaker area to the wind. On this boat the heel end is on a saddle (fig 7-23) which can slide up the mast even though the sideways pressure from the pole under load is considerable.

Pole position

The pole is first positioned as close as possible to 90 degrees across the apparent wind. The sheet can then be hauled in until the spinnaker fills. The sheet must then be eased until the luff of the spinnaker folds in. A sharp tug is all that is needed to make the luff stand again. With the sail full the height of the tack must now be adjusted by raising or lowering the pole to set the spinnaker up squarely into the wind. The popular rule for optimum pole height is to keep the tack of the sail

fig 7-23

level with the clew. Because the wind blows parallel to the water, boat heel often complicates this and it is a mistake to follow the method too rigidily.

On some spinnakers the position at which the luff first folds is a useful guide to correct pole height. The sail is working in exactly the same way as a headsail. If the top folds first (fig 7-24 (a)) the *clew* is too high: raise the pole. If the lower luff collapses before the upper (b), lower the pole. For spinnakers where this technique works the break point should be just above mid-luff (c). The spinnaker is then trimmed to its optimum, but it cannot be over-emphasized how important it is to keep the sail on the verge of collapsing along its luff. Only in this way is it possible to maximize the forward pulling component of its total effort whatever the wind direction.

This can clearly be seen on a close reach by observing the angle made by the halyard where it exits from the mast, relative to the direction of the boat. A very small easing of the sheet will have a marked effect on the amount the halyard swings forward to pull in the same direction as the boat. In both cases the spinnaker would look to be drawing powerfully.

Spinnaker shape, because of the distorted perspectives encountered when viewed from deck level, is certainly the most difficult to evaluate correctly. A very common complaint to sailmakers is that 'my spinnaker is nowhere near as

fig 7-24 (a, b, c)

dinghy this means that the guy and sheet are constantly swinging the sail around an arc in front of the mast. On displacement boats it is thought wiser to ignore small variations in the wind direction as far as the pole position is concerned, in favour of retaining an undisturbed flow in the sail. Even when pole adjustment becomes necessary it should be done slowly and smoothly for the same reason.

At all times during a run the aim should be to get the spinnaker to fly as high as possible, so giving it an opportunity to open its wings (fig 7-26). In heavy weather this becomes even more important on a dinghy or small non-masthead boat where for 'spreading its wings' read 'opening the leech', to allow excess flow to escape. On a reach this

fig 7-26

fig 7.25

large or as full as the rest of the fleet'. It is of course; it is simply a question of where you view it from! Compare (fig 7-25) with the three views from the helmsmans position. Same spinnaker, same wind, same point of sailing. Only the viewing angle has changed.

As the wind or boat direction varies so the pole must be kept at 90 degrees to the apparent wind, and the sheet trimming process is repeated. On a

flattening effect in the top part of the sails can be aided by moving the fairlead aft. This technique equally applies to yacht spinnakers, other than Starcut, on a reach, although here the aim is to allow the clew to rise above the level of the tack which has been pulled down to straighten out the luff. The leech falls off spilling air and decreasing the angle of heel.

The difficulties of running in heavy weather on a yacht can best be countered by effectively reducing the area of sail. Once past the need to generate power, but rather to survive, strapping the sail

fig 7-27

down with sheet and guy led from fairleads adjacent to the mast reduces area (fig 7-27), restrains the sail from swinging laterally, and the sheets themselves exert their pull on a point which steers the boat forward rather than wrenching it sideways.

Launching chutes

With most dinghies and small keelboats now equipped with spinnaker launching chutes, getting the sail up and down is simplicity itself (fig 7-28). The halyard and downhaul can be a continuous line leading from the head of the sail through the sheave near the hounds, down to an exit at the heel, back to the helm position; returning to the bow where it emerges through the chute entry and is fastened to a strengthened patch in the middle of the spinnaker.

The downhaul must lead up in front of the spinnaker foot (red broken line), rather than behind it. It then divides the foot when pulled down allowing the sail to be nearly dragged into the chute. Were it to pull down from the aft side of the sail, the foot could easily drop over the bow. Whether the downhaul is attached to one patch equidistant between head, tack and clew (fig 7-29 (a)), or laces through a lower cringle before being attached to a patch higher up the sail (b) depends on the space available for storage below decks. If space is restricted the latter method gets over the problem. The distance between the head and the upper fixing point, the distance between both tack and clew and the lower cringle, and the available stowing length (red) must all be equal. Otherwise when pulled down the head, tack and clew will not come together neatly ready to be re-launched.

fig 7-28

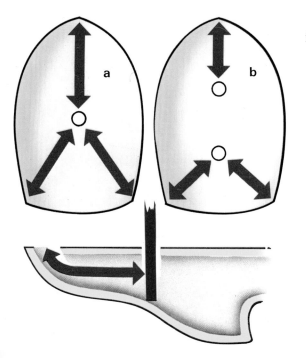

fig 7-29

fig 7-30

fig 7-31

Turtles

Spinnakers on larger boats and those without launching chutes, can be hoisted from under the headsail; from a turtle in the pulpit or if crew movement is restricted from a bag aft of the foresail.

The first method is popular because whilst the spinnaker is being hoisted it is blanketed by the headsail (fig 7-30). Furthermore if launched from a three hole turtle, the leads tend to straighten out any twists in the nylon sail as it slides up over the leeward surface of the headsail. Spinnakers have understandably a reputation for being difficult to manage. This has led, from time to time, to the appearance on the market of various tubes and squeezers designed to make launching and re-covery more controllable. This may be the case, but from experience, it would seem that the quickest method of raising and lowering a spinnaker is both the easiest and the most convenient.

Lowering a spinnaker usually involves releasing one of its attached lower points, thereby spilling all of the air from the sail. On ocean racers it will be the tack which is released. The pole is lowered and hauled forward so that a foredeck hand can reach a special snap shackle (fig 7-31) designed to release under load. The sail flutters aft and is recovered via the sheet under the blanketing mainsail, whilst the halyard is eased at a controlled rate to stop the spinnaker ending up in the water (fig 7-32).

This system has been improved in some racing yachts whose skippers prefer not to have a large spinnaker flying around, particularly when rounding buoys at close quarters with other boats. They attach a short retrieving line to the tack. This is then led below the foot of the hoisted headsail. As the tack is released from the boom, so the sheet is

fig 7-33

also eased and the spinnaker drawn in under the headsail on to the foredeck.

It is worth noting here that unlike genoa sheets, the spinnaker sheet and guys *should never have knots* in their inboard ends. In an emergency, either can then be run through their fairleads spilling all wind out of the sail.

Before repacking, if the sail is to come out of its bag without twists next time, it must be 'refolded' correctly. This is done by two crew each running one hand along opposite sides of the sail, collecting the tape in large folds in their other hands (fig 7-33). Once the head and both tack/clew rings are together the body of the sail can be stuffed into the bag, leaving the attachment points until last on top of the rebagged sail.

fig 7-32

fig 7-34

Big-boy/Blooper

No review of modern spinnaker techniques would be complete without mention of the blooper (or big-boy, or shooter) (fig 7-34).

The big-boy first appeared in the early 1970s originally as an ordinary genoa exploiting the rating rule by those seeking extra downwind sail area. Its appearance was greeted with cries of 'unseamanlike' due to the apparent unwieldy bulk of the sail. Ironically it is now alleged to be important as a balancing sail for unwieldy spinnakers, as it is a means of extending the available flow area. It can sometimes diminish the eagerness to broach displayed by the average modern offshore racing yacht, and also achieves reduction in the tendency to roll when on a near dead run.

As the fine curves of both luff and leech of the blooper have developed quickly, so have the techniques for trimming and handling. It must be clearly understood however what the blooper is setting out to achieve. It is a means of extending the leech of the spinnaker out past the shadow of the mainsail to attract flow into both itself and the spinnaker. The head of the blooper is also complementing that of the spinnaker deflecting wind into vertical flow.

Under current rules the luff length of the sail is restricted to less than that of the spinnaker. Neither can it be supported away from the boat with a pole.

It must therefore be coaxed to fly out into the same plane as the spinnaker if it is to play an effective complementary role.

The blooper is hoisted on a spare halyard which has first been passed outside the spinnaker sheet (fig 7-35). The tack of the sail is made fast to a cleat on the bow with a short strop which leads in through the foreward life lines. Once hoisted and full of wind, both sheet and halyard should be eased as far as each will go before the sail collapses (fig 7-36). They must then be constantly played together in much the same way as the luff of the spinnaker is kept just on the verge of collapse. Whilst the blooper may look all-powerful, unless the halyard and sheet are eased to this optimum, it could easily be doing more harm than good by interfering with the flow around and over the spinnaker.

fig 7-35

fig 7-36

Index